# The Road She Walked

## One woman's journey of resilience and faith

**CAMETA SENIOR**

# The Road She Walked

One Woman's Journey of Resilience and Faith

*Copyright © 2020 Cameta Senior*

ISBN 978-1-5272-7342-9

Memoir, Christian, Personal Growth

Published in the United Kingdom

Independently published with support from The Editor's Chair

# ACKNOWLEDGEMENTS

### To Andrea Thompson,

My beautiful daughter, thank you for encouraging me all the way. Thank you for the late nights and the assistance you gave me. You said, 'Mum you can do it, I'm proud of you.'

### To Dean,

My son, thank you for pushing me to pursue my dreams and allowing me to reach my full potential.

### To Eddie Goss,

Thank you for being an amazing friend to me for the last 20 years. Thank you for encouraging me to write this book and helping me to make my dreams come true, through all the ups and downs.

### To Daphne Briscoe,

Thank you for your support as I was writing this book. Our bond goes back to the time we were ordained together as missionaries, and now we are prayer partners.

### To Valerie Bailey and Wayne Thompson,

To my sister, Valerie, and brother, Wayne, thank you both for supporting me while I was writing this book.

### To Joan Prince,

A sister-friend who looked after me while I was ill. Thank you for being a tower of strength to me and the family.

# A WORD
## FROM THE **AUTHOR**

I decided to write a book about my life and the things that I have experienced as a way to help someone. I hope that it will inspire and make a difference in someone's life. Some people see me as very simple, dyslexic, and not well educated, but God saw something in me and gave me the confidence to do what I thought was impossible. God didn't write me off but showed His unconditional love towards me. Writing this book has been an eye-opener; it has allowed me to overcome my fears, and I will never allow myself to be discouraged by others again.

This will go down as one of my achievements and will always remind me that, 'I can do all things through Christ that strengthens me.'

*Cameta*

# RECOMMENDATIONS

I have found writing this very hard because when I think back over the years I've known Cameta, I could write pages! Anyway, I will try and condense what I have to say about this very dear and special lady.

I met Cameta in my late teens when our youth leader at the time decided it would be good for the group to be divided into "prayer partners" as a way to encourage us to pray for and strengthen one another. I was paired with Cameta and I wasn't too happy about it! Although I thought she was nice, I had formed some opinions about her and told her something to that effect at our first meeting.

Whatever I said didn't put her off and she scheduled the meetings at her home, so I attended. I realised that this young married woman with a young family really did pray regularly; she actually liked praying, and God answered.

From that time on, over the years, Cameta has been an advisor, counsellor, even a mentor to me. Above all, she's been a friend. We have had times where we laughed till we cried and times where we cried till we laughed. I can ask her anything. I have found that what I've learned from reading books, Cameta naturally thinks that way.

Am I glad Cameta has written a book? Yes, and 100 times, yes! I am so proud of her and I am privileged to have been a witness to some of the journey you will read in the following pages. I hope you will be encouraged through the laughter and the tears. Blessings

*Beverly Mayers*

I have known Cameta since way back when we were young people growing up in church. Growing up I saw her as a very spiritual person with a love for the Lord. Cameta has been through many challenges, times of despair, sickness and loss. But as the songwriter states, through it all, she has learned to trust in God. In her darkest times she cried out and God heard her cry and delivered her from all her fears. This book is borne out of a desire for Cameta to share her life experiences of triumph over adversity with others who might find comfort and encouragement from her story. This is the story of her life growing up in the Caribbean, being left behind when her parents moved to Britain to start new lives, and eventually joining them and having to settle in a strange land. This is the story of her experiences along the way, the repercussions and her resilience as she has had to encounter and overcome the challenges that came her way. I find it inspiring and pray you will too.

*Elaine Vassell*

# CONTENTS

THE ROAD SHE WALKED

# CHAPTER ONE

# My CHILDHOOD IN JAMAICA

I'm about to take you on a journey of my life, which is full of many highs and lows. I hope you have a sense of humour too, as I'm sure you'll find a few things to laugh about.

It all began on Wednesday 3rd of December 1958 when I, Cameta Rosealee Thompson, was born to Albert and Clarice Thompson in Christiana, parish of Manchester, Jamaica.

I was the sixth child, after Philip, Violet (also known as Vie or Valerie), Cherry, Lee and Pauline. In total there were to be nine of us. Wayne, Jeffeth and Sonia would follow after me. However, only eight of us survived, as Lee unfortunately passed away before his first birthday.

I was a little redhead girl, full of fun and joy. I had a very good sense of humour and I was always up to tricks. You would only have to look at me with my red hair and a cheeky smile on my face and you would have laughed.

We lived in a two-room, board house with a zinc roof. We had a front room and one bedroom. The bedroom was my parents' room, and at night the front room became the bedroom for the children. The house was raised on four cement blocks, and we had three steps up to the entrance. The kitchen was outside and so was the toilet. Under the house was a cellar that was used for storage.

## Mast Amos

My grandmother on my father's side lived very far from us. Whenever she would visit, she would come with a basket on her head bringing lots of our favourite fruits, such as mangoes, bananas, sweet sap and naseberries, which we called 'goodies'. We looked forward to her visits and whenever she couldn't make it, she would send her son, Mast Amos (my uncle), to bring the goodies.

Whenever he came over, my uncle would call me aside to come and sit on his knee with my mango and while everyone was distracted by the excitement of picking and eating what they wanted, he would be playing with me inappropriately. I was about six years old the last time Mast Amos visited our house. He brought the goodies and did the usual thing of telling me to come and sit on his knee. While everyone was under the spell of excitement about all the goodies he had brought, he was rubbing me down and trying to put his hand under my dress. After I ate my mango, I got off his knee and went and told my dad what he had done.

My dad called him and asked what he was doing, to which he replied, 'What do you mean, my brother?'

'Cam told me you were putting your hands under her dress,' my dad replied. When my uncle denied this my dad called me and asked me to repeat what I had said.

I replied boldly, 'Every time Mast Amos comes to visit us, he rubs me down but today he put his hand under my dress.' The next thing I knew was my dad had punched him to the point that he dropped to the ground. He told him never to step foot on his land again. I didn't see my uncle again until I was about 17 years old and sometime after that I learnt that he passed away.

It was only later in life that I realised that this was child abuse. Being so young I didn't really understand what he was really doing, but when he put his hand under my dress, I knew that was wrong.

## Dad goes to 'Foreign'

One day soon afterwards, we had a prayer meeting. It started with my mum praying, followed by the children saying the 'Our Father' prayer. Dad was the last to pray. Unbeknownst to me, this would be the last I would see of him for a very long time. With eight of us children to feed, things had become hard for us financially, so Dad had decided to leave his family to seek a better life for us in England (which we called 'Foreign').

After a few days I asked Mum where Dad was and she replied, 'Cam, your Daddy is in Foreign.'

'Where is Foreign?' I asked.

'A very long way away,' she said.

'Is it in the sky?' I asked.

'No,' she replied, 'but a very long way away.'

'Will I ever see him again?'

'I hope so,' Mum replied. This made me happy to know that one day I would see him again.

Now that Dad was in England, Mum took on a job to help to bring in some money. She would wash and iron clothes for Miss Vera, who was elderly and needed assistance. The wages she received were almost enough to buy us food and household essentials.

On Sundays, Mum would make sure we all got dressed up in our Sunday best and were early for church.

My sisters and I loved to put on our pretty dresses. I remember wearing a white lace dress with white ankle socks, and black shoes, with my hair done up with ribbons and bobbles. On Sundays, I would always feel special, as I was dressed like a princess. I felt as though no one could touch me on a Sunday, and I always tried to be on my best behaviour.

The second row was where I always sat in church, right next to Mum. I would enjoy the singing and clapping but would get bored and fall asleep when the preacher started speaking. Mum would keep nudging me to wake me up. I would always ask to go pee-pee, but she knew I just wanted to go outside. She would tell me no and say, 'Keep quiet and sit down, you do not want to go pee-pee.'

I remember one day I asked to go to the post office with my mum, only so I could get a patty and a soda. I would live to regret this. Mum spoke to every person she passed on the way and I was getting bored. It was taking such a long time for me to get this patty and soda. Eventually, we got to the post office only to find the longest queue ever. I thought we would never reach the counter, but when we did, Mum gave her name only to be told there were no letters that day. This was such a disappointment for both of us. This meant I wasn't going to get a patty and a soda. Perhaps seeing my disappointment, Mum scraped together enough to at least get me a patty. This was all she could afford as she still had to buy dinner for that day.

That evening for dinner we had a piece of white yam, one dumpling each, some callaloo cooked up with onion and tomato and 'no salting' (which means no meat). We washed that down with some sugar and water with 'bugga lime'.

## School

I can clearly remember my first day at school. I got all dressed up in my blue tunic and white shirt and thought I looked very pretty in my uniform.

I went to Zoan Primary School, which was only a short walking distance from my home. My mum took me to school for the first two days, where she met my teacher, Miss Gail. I only attended half days, from 9 am to 12 noon. I looked forward to going to school and soon became best friends with Joy, who lived two streets away from me. I remember thinking that the classroom was so huge, with long wooden benches and wooden desks. When I looked across the room, I saw a long bamboo stick hanging on the wall in the corner. I would soon learn that this was the cane. It was only used if you were late for school, didn't listen to the teacher, or if you were caught fighting. The teacher reminded us every morning about this instrument of punishment. There would be many times when I would get the cane, or witness somebody else getting it.

On the other side of the classroom were a Jamaican flag and some pictures of Jamaica's heroes. My favourite was one of Marcus Garvey because he had fought for people's freedom.

The playground was huge. It had four toilets, two for the boys and two for the girls. There were some big stones that looked like chairs that we could sit on, and we had two big shelter areas that we would sit under whenever it rained. Our playtime was only fifteen minutes – then we had to get back to class. We had to work on counting and spelling. Soon after that, it would be home time. Mum would be waiting for me by the water pipe and I always looked forward to seeing her and going home.

## Mum Goes to 'Foreign'

It was a Sunday afternoon. After church we came home and sat down to have dinner, when Mum said she had something to tell us. I thought it was good news that Dad was coming home, but it wasn't. It was bad news, as she told us she was going to join Dad in England. I remember one of my sisters asking how long she would be gone, to which she replied, 'Don't worry, we will send for you all.'

I started to cry saying, 'Not again! Why do you have to go as well? Who will look after us?'

Mum replied, 'Your Grandma Ethelyn,' (my mother's mother). When the day arrived and Mum took us to my Grandma Ethelyn, who lived in Fairfield, I cried all the way there. My sister Cherry said, 'Stop crying, Cam, you will see Mum again.' I cried more, and Cherry hugged me. It felt good but I still felt pain deep in my heart. Mum was going away.

As she was leaving, my mum hugged each one of us, but I held onto her and cried. We all cried. This was the last time I saw my mum before she left to go to England around 1963.

Living with Grandma, everything changed. I started at a new school called Linken Fairfield Primary School. I had a new uniform, new teachers, new friends, and I just had to go with the flow. My sisters Pauline, Vie and Cherry were happy with our new environment, but I wasn't. They would take me home from school so that Grandma didn't have to come for me. My two little brothers, Wayne and Jeffeth, were at home with my grandma as they were still too young for school.

I could not settle down in school because I was missing Mum. I would take my frustration out on the other children. I felt that no one understood me. I would fight every day and cry and tell the children all the bad Jamaican words that I knew. I was hurting, but no one ever asked me why I was doing this. Sometimes at school, my sister Cherry would let me start a fight and she would finish it. We had a name in the school – the 'Thompson Conquerors'. It meant no one could beat us. I would fight with my slate and it would break, then I would hide it from Grandma.

But one day when I was going home, I met Grandma along the road and she saw me with the slate before I could hide it. With the look she gave me, I knew that a beating was coming, and come it did! It was my fault so I could not do anything about it. But every time I got a new slate, I would still use it to fight. This was my weapon.

Eventually, Grandma asked, 'Cam, why you keep doing that? It cost money to buy these slates! You don't care?'

I answered, 'No, Grandma, I don't care.'

This got Grandma mad. She said, 'What is the problem?'

'I want my mum!'

'She's gone to get a good job and a better place for you all,' Grandma explained. The next day I went to school without my slate. When the teacher asked me where it was, I told her it was broken.

'Well, today you are going to write out of your hand middle,' she told me. So, I had to sit and just listen to the teacher. Fortunately, I didn't have to write 'out of my hand middle' for real, plus Dad sent some money that week so I got a new slate. This was a nice one. It had a frame with an abacus on the bottom and because I liked it, I didn't use it to fight. It now just meant that I would have to use my fists, kick, and bite instead. Most of the children were afraid of me, and I couldn't blame them.

Grandma was fed up with my behaviour at school, but what could the poor woman do? Sometimes my sister Cherry was unable to be at school because she had to go to the market with my grandma to sell carrots. During these times I would fight more. When my sisters were at school I would try to behave, especially when Cherry was there.

When we came home from school, we all had our little chores to do in the evenings before dinner and bedtime. I would have to take off my uniform and re-iron it with a piece of white cloth to keep the pleats, I'd also have to wash my white blouse and my socks ready for the morning. After that, I would sweep half of the yard (it was too big for me to sweep on my own) and then go and look for wood for the fire for cooking. I would then go down to the pipe to get water with my sisters. Each evening Mast Brother (Grandma's husband) would wait for Grandma to finish cooking, so that he could go and cook his own pot. He would boil about 20 dumplings at a time. My sister Cherry would be in the house, and use a long stick to take out three or four of his dumplings through the window. When she got the dumplings, we would hide them in our water pan and eat them on the way to get the water.

When we got home my grandma's husband would ask, 'Which one of you girls did this?' and we would say we didn't know. When he didn't cook, we would find ways to pick people's mangoes and oranges off their trees. This made life fun and helped me to enjoy my jobs. While waiting for dinner to cook, I would play hopscotch with my sisters or marbles with my brothers.

One night we waited a very long time for dinner. The fire would not light because the wood was so cold. We blew so much we started coughing. The smoke was bad but we got it going in the end. Our stove was four stones with three iron bars across. There was a table in the corner for preparing food, some pots hanging up on the wall and a small window.

When it was time to get ready for bed, we had our wash in a big tub. Grandma would come into the room and ask, 'You all ready to say prayers?' We all had to say our prayers. There were two prayers that we regularly said. Mine was 'Pray Mama and pray Papa, pray that God will help and keep me through the night'. The other prayer we often said was, 'Gentle Jesus, meek and mild, look upon a little child. Amen'.

## The Miracle

One day we came home from school and Grandma said, 'We need a miracle today.' I wondered what she meant. I soon learned there was no food in the house to cook. My grandma was a woman of God. When she prayed, God answered her. She called Pauline to put the pot on the fire, but there was nothing in the pot, just water. The water boiled until it dried out, then she told Pauline to put more water in the pot. We all thought, 'What is she doing?' About half an hour later a man called Mr Brown came to the house carrying a basket on his head. He called my grandma and said he had brought some food for her. Mr Brown did not know what was happening, he did not know we had no food to eat. God had answered Grandma's prayer! The food came at the right time for us. That night we had dinner – saltfish, cooked up with onion and tomatoes, yam, banana, dasheen and sweet potato. Grandma said, 'Give thanks,' and we all did. From that day onwards we always had food. Someone always passed by and blessed us.

When things began to get hard, my sister Cherry would go to the market with my aunt to sell carrots, and bring the money to Grandma. This helped us get by. It taught us that prayer worked and that it is good to trust in God. As a child, this reminded me that when you pray, God answers, and that has stayed with me forever. It taught me to have faith in God as my grandma did, for that is how she lived her life – by trusting in God.

When I saw how God worked, I began to ask questions about Him. I asked, 'Grandma, how did you meet God?'

'Child, it is a long story,' she replied. Then she began to tell me part of the story even though she said I might not understand it all. Her faith had been handed down from her mother who was also a praying woman. Grandma saw that prayer worked and that's how she started to believe.

I asked, 'Where does God live?'

'Heaven.'

'Where, in the sky?'

'No,' Grandma replied. 'Heaven is a long way away. I have never seen God but I have felt His presence.'

'Is He a duppy?' (a type of spirit).

Grandma laughed and said, 'My child, He is something like that but He is not a ghost.'

I had more questions. 'Can you see Him?' I asked.

'No,' she said.

'He sounds very scary,' I concluded.

So, that night when we read the Bible, Grandma opened the book of Revelation, chapter 1:14 and 15, so she could show me what God is like.

She read, 'His hair was white like wool, as white as snow, and His eyes were like flames of fire. His feet were like fine brass as if they were burnt in a furnace; and His voice sounds like many waters.' It was quite enough for me!

'I don't want to meet Him,' I said. 'He is very scary! Can He see me?'

'Yes, He can see you everywhere you go.'

So, right then, I tried to hide my face so God couldn't see me. I told Grandma, 'I think I will love God, but I will stay away from Him.'

She simply said, 'Come Cam, it is time to go to bed.'

Grandma continued to look after us for a while after that. One day, my sisters noticed that she did not look herself. This went on for a while and so they began to watch her. They realised she was not well and took her to the doctor. Remembering what Grandma had taught me about God, I began to pray. I asked God not to let my grandma die, and He answered my prayer.

Whenever she was feeling pain, Mast Brother would sing to her over and over again. I remember the song to this day. It went like this: 'I want to go home and live with my Saviour and friend, and to be with Him there until the end of my journey is done.'

Mast Brother was a quiet man and did not speak much. He was a shoemaker. Sometimes he would put two pieces of leather together and make a musical instrument. While he played and sang, I would sing as well to make my grandma happy.

I was really happy when Grandma began feeling better. We were all happy. Soon she was back on her feet again and doing what she used to do. Boy, did I praise God!

When we went to church, I used to hold her hand and Grandma would say, 'Cam, you are a special little girl. You are very caring and you will make people happy. May God bless you, my child.'

When an elderly person says you're blessed, you are truly blessed! Shortly after that, it was almost time for Christmas. A barrel from England was coming in a few days and I was looking forward to my present.

It was a Monday morning when we heard the sound of the truck coming around the corner. We were happy because we knew it was stopping at our house, which it did. Two men came out and called for my grandma. She came out of the house and after they had checked her name, they left the barrel on the veranda. We were excited the barrel had arrived, but Grandma wouldn't let us open it because Christmas was still a few days away.

On Christmas morning, Grandma opened the barrel and gave everyone their presents. Wayne and Jeffeth got the cars they wanted. I had asked for a dolly because the one I had was made from a mango seed. When I saw my dolly, I was so disappointed because it couldn't do anything. It was a porcelain doll, and its hands were stuck by its sides, and its legs were stuck together too. Only its eyes moved, so I took it and smashed it in pieces! And got a very good beating from my grandma, who sent me to bed telling me how ungrateful I was, because my parents had worked hard to send it. Despite all that, we had a lovely Christmas.

Shortly afterwards, Grandma became ill again, too ill to look after us, so we had to go and live with our Aunty May (my dad's sister). She came to collect us and that was the last time I saw Grandma.

# CHAPTER TWO

# Coming
## TO ENGLAND

'Stop crying,' Pauline told me, 'or you'll make me cry too.'
We had all been bundled into a car and were on our way
to Aunty May's house. I tried my best to do as my sister
Pauline said and to stop crying, but it wasn't easy. I felt sad to be
leaving Grandma.

As we drove away, I looked back at the house and at the mango trees
where we had so often feasted. I looked at all the special landmarks,
the church and the school I went to. Inside, I knew that this would
be the last time I would see this place. We got to a crossroads where
I saw two of my friends, and I waved goodbye to them. They didn't
know that I was leaving and probably thought I was just waving to
say hello, but that was the last time I saw them, too.

After driving for what felt like two hours, we arrived back in
Christiana. The car stopped outside a large white house. It was
the biggest house I had ever seen; it had six bedrooms. This was
Aunty May's house, our new home. The yard was enormous. On
the right-hand side of the house was a big white tomb, on the left-
hand side was a flower garden and behind that were lots of fruit
trees bearing bananas, pears and oranges.

Only four people were living in the house before we arrived there.
There was Aunty May, her daughter Joy, our cousin Charmaine
and the gardener, who lived in the basement. I shared a room

with Charmaine while my sisters Cherry and Pauline shared a room. My two brothers, Wayne and Jeffeth, shared the fourth bedroom.

We quickly settled in. I remember thinking how strange it felt to feel both happy and sad at the same time. I was sad about leaving Grandma's house, yet happy to be staying in this big white house. My room was big enough to hold two beds and two chests of drawers. This was the first time I would sleep in a bed by myself. I remember being called to dinner for the first time there. We all sat around the big wooden dining table. Aunty May had prepared one of my favourite meals: oxtail with butter beans, rice and peas. We washed that down with a beverage of sugar and water, flavoured with bugga lime. Once dinner was over, Aunty May gave us our chores. I had the worst job of all! I had to empty the chimmys (potties). I had to wash them at the back of the house then turn them upside down to dry on the big white tomb. Later, I had to replace them under the beds for the night.

I used to love to play in the big yard in front of the house. I would play marbles, hopscotch and hide-and-seek with my two brothers. One day, while playing hide-and-seek, I hid behind a tree. I was standing on a stone when suddenly I felt my feet rising from the ground. Looking down, I saw that I was standing on an enormous bullfrog! I screamed, and ran crying to my brothers. After this, I refused to play outside for a long while.

## Going to 'Foreign'

One June day, Cherry decided to take me with her on one of her many visits to the post office. This was the time of year we often referred to as mango season, because we used to pick people's mangos from their trees on the way to and from home. I didn't enjoy going to the post office as it meant a lot of waiting around in queues. When we finally got to the counter, we gave them my aunt's name. They checked to see whether we had any post and came back with just one letter. We realised that it was from our parents and thought they had sent us money. We rushed home to give the letter to my aunt. She must have read the letter on her own at first, because I remember that she called the three of us girls – Cherry, Pauline, and myself – to her room and informed us that we would be going to live with our parents in England.

'What about Wayne and Jeffeth?' Pauline asked.

'They will follow you shortly,' Aunty May replied.

I was so happy to hear this news that we were going to England. I couldn't wait to see my parents again. It must have been at least two years since I had last seen them. I remember Aunty May going to sort out our passports and taking us to the dressmaker where we had matching dresses made. All that the three of us girls could think and talk about was the trip to England. We were so excited! Of course, Wayne and Jeffeth were a little sad that we were leaving, but they were consoled by the promise that they would follow behind us shortly.

I had heard quite a bit about England from my sister Violet, otherwise known as Vie, who had been the first of my siblings to come to England in 1964 at the age of fifteen. She would write to us and tell us about life at Brixton College, which she attended when she turned seventeen. She did not like England and described it as being so icy that one day on her way from college, she was not able to feel her face: her fingers were so cold they became numb. Then her teeth began to chatter. She looked up to see cold white fluff falling from the sky. Quickly, she had gone home to tell Mum that cold, white bread was falling from the sky. My mum had laughed and told her it was snow. When she awoke the next morning, the road and houses were all covered in snow. She said it looked beautiful but was freezing cold. She said she didn't like walking in the snow or hearing the crunching sound it made under her feet. Vie had to wear boots, a coat and gloves to college, and it was all new to her coming from Jamaica.

The day finally arrived for us to leave Jamaica and we said goodbye to Wayne, Jeffeth, Joy, Charmaine and the gardener and set off for Kingston Airport. There were butterflies in my belly as we arrived with Aunty May and proceeded to go inside. I remember seeing so many people and lots of queues. It was extremely busy. My aunty took us to a short queue where she checked us in and handed us over to a chaperone. As we said our goodbyes, Aunty May said, 'God go with you all.' We were sad to leave our aunty but happy to be going to join our parents.

The chaperone took us to the departure lounge, and it was at this point that I saw the aeroplane up close for the first time. It seemed huge! We were shown to our seats where we all sat together. When I looked around, I couldn't believe that so many people were going to fit on the aeroplane along with all the luggage. I began wondering how the plane was going to stay up in the sky! We were told to put on our seatbelts and the plane started to take off. It began moving slowly, then faster and I realised that we were in the air. Suddenly feeling very scared, I prayed that God would carry us safely to England.

Though scary, the plane ride was a fun experience. We watched a movie on a big TV screen and the huge fluffy clouds outside the window. When the air hostess brought us our food and drink, I didn't like it. Pauline told me to eat it or I would be hungry because we wouldn't get anything else to eat until we arrived in England. But I wouldn't. It didn't look or smell like my rice and peas or dumplings back home; it looked horrible. I thought this was probably what the food looked like in England.

When I needed to go to the toilet, Pauline came with me but we didn't know how to open the door, so a passenger had to come and help us. When I flushed the toilet, it made a noise so loud that I thought the plane was going to crash!

Several hours later we arrived in England. I was happy to have arrived safely and to be getting off the plane. Just before I stepped off, I felt the cold, damp air and noticed how everything looked dull and grey. This was not what I had expected Great Britain to look like. It felt disappointing to have left sunny Jamaica to come to this cold, dreary place. The chaperone took us to a meeting point, where we waited a few minutes before I saw my mother walking quickly towards us.

'Mamma's coming!' I cried excitedly to my sisters.

'That's not Mamma,' one of them replied, but it was. They hardly recognised her as she had put on weight, but I had not forgotten her face.

She was coming with someone who I at first thought was my dad. He was a mixed-race man, and I had heard a rumour that when you go to England you become white, but I soon learned that he was just Brother Gordon, a family friend.

I ran and hugged my mum and was so excited to be reunited with her. My mum was so happy to have us back and gave us all a hug. I then think the shock of our outfits kicked in.

She greeted us but then after the chaperone had handed us over to her, she turned to her friend and said, 'Throw dem in the car before anyone sees them!' She was not impressed with our colourful outfits at all. We were dressed liked triplets, we had on blue and pink dresses, with a blue and pink turban and a pearl hanging down on our forehead. The dresses were pink in the middle and had blue side panels, and the turban was the same design.

On the drive home, I took in my first sights of Great Britain. I noticed that the buildings looked like factories and marvelled at how close together they all were. I didn't realise at the time that all those small compact buildings were houses, and that I was going to live in one of them. Finally, we pulled up outside a grey house in Brixton, London. There was no big yard for me to play in and inside was just as disappointing: it was so small. We were led into the front room which was a pretty, clean room, well furnished with a television set, gram and sofa. On one of the walls was a plaque with the words 'Bless this house'. There were loads of ornaments and the chairs and sofa had lacy crocheted covers on their backs. There was a cabinet with drinking glasses and dinnerware. Overall, it was pleasant but very different from Jamaica.

After that first day, we were only allowed to go into the front room for two occasions: whenever my parents' friends came over or when we had to clean it. It was a special room reserved for visitors. We gathered and watched television in the dining room instead.

I remember when my dad came home from work, he walked in and said something along the lines of, 'Hi everyone, I'm your dad,' and I said, 'I thought you would be white.' He turned to me and said, 'Hold on, I soon come.' He went upstairs to change his clothes and came back in a white overall and cream on his face and said, 'Do I look white now?' I then swore at him, to which he turned to my mum and said, 'This one is going to be trouble.' Our parents' friends and other relatives came over that week to meet us; we received a warm welcome from them. They seemed happy that we had come to live in England. The hub of our community was the church, which we attended every Sunday. The worship reminded me of the church I had been to in Jamaica with my grandma – I enjoyed the singing, clapping and loud preaching as it took me back to my roots. This helped me to settle into my new country.

## School in the UK

Soon it was time for my parents to find a school for me. My sister Cherry went to Brixton College, while Pauline went to Priory Park Secondary School. I went to Richard Atkinson Primary School on New Park Road. Unfortunately, I didn't do very well there. I was separated from my sisters and felt alone. I started fighting with everyone who came near me, even the teachers. As I couldn't speak the Queen's English and didn't understand the English accent, the other children laughed and picked on me. They would call me names and ask what language I spoke. I would tell them I spoke Patois but this made them laugh even harder because they'd never heard of it.

This is where the trouble began. I wasn't going to stand for anyone laughing at me and I didn't understand them, so rather than ask questions I just started fighting them. This time, I had no one to help me fight as I was on my own, but I was not afraid of anyone. My parents were often called to the school. It was always Mum who came; my dad did not come, not even once. He was ashamed of me but I did not care; I just wanted to go back to Jamaica to my grandma. When Mum would come to my school, they told her that they thought I had behavioural problems. They thought I needed to go to a specialist school where they'd be better equipped to cope with me and where I could get the assistance I needed.

Luckily, I was only in this school for a year as I was now eleven years old and in my final year of primary school. This meant that my parents had to find a secondary school for me. First, I went to my sister Pauline's school but only for a short time. I found it difficult to do the work there because I could not read or write properly. It was my secret. In Jamaica, I hadn't always been sent to school because there hadn't always been enough money. Only the older ones had been sent to school regularly.

I was assigned a key worker, who was supposed to help me find a new school and help during my lessons too. It turned out that she felt that Turney School in Dulwich was where I needed to be as it was a school for children with learning difficulties.

Mum was happy to hear the news that a school had been found. As soon as she saw the headmaster she said, 'Mi spirit take to him,' and that was that. The headmaster, Mr Ray, was kind to Mum and me and we both felt comfortable with him. He explained to my mum that I needed to take a test because although my behaviour qualified me, I still needed to be assessed.

When the day of the test arrived, my mum and I were nervous but they told us that it would only take half an hour. I timidly entered a huge white room with large tables in the middle. I saw three scary-looking men and a woman, all wearing white coats and sitting around a desk. The woman said, 'Hello, Cameta, just do what we ask.' These people frightened me with their serious faces and their coats that reminded me of doctors.

On the table was a tray of red, green and yellow bricks. The woman asked, 'Can you see these bricks?' I knew that these doctors thought I was crazy, so I decided to show them just how crazy I really was. When the red light came on, I picked up the red brick. Then I proceeded to throw the bricks one by one at the doctors. I even picked up the tray and hurled that at them, too. It was kind of funny to see their shocked faces, and I laughed and laughed. Of course, they were all very concerned and Mum was shocked and embarrassed. Surprisingly, she didn't punish me for my bad behaviour. The doctors stopped the session, told Mum they'd let her know their decision and then we were free to leave.

I think I had acted out that way because I'd overheard one of the doctors saying that if I passed the test, I'd be able to go to one of the other schools. I didn't want this, though. I really wanted to go to Turney because I liked Mr Ray. He was caring and kind and I felt safe with him.

Mum and I laughed about the incident on the way home. 'Oh, Cam, you're too bad!' she said. I told her that I liked Mr Ray and she agreed.

Mr Ray himself called a while later and told Mum that he was accepting me into Turney. The poor man didn't know what he was letting himself in for because – although I liked him – at first, I was nothing but trouble.

The school bus picked me up the following Monday morning. I remember that it was a blue and white bus with funny looking children inside. Some of them were disabled and some were rocking back and forth making strange noises. I found this very disturbing and decided that there was no way I was going to use that school bus. I was worried that my friends would think that there was something wrong with me so after a few days I told my mum that my teacher had said I could take the red bus. I used to get off two stops after my school so that nobody could see what school I was attending.

Most days, I was not happy to be in school. We had to attend boring assemblies, where they sang boring songs and said long, boring prayers. I found all the lessons tedious, too. There was simply nothing fun about being in school, and half the time I didn't even listen but instead thought of ways to get out of going. There were lots of other black children at the school at this time too. Many of them were Jamaican and they also spoke with an accent.

On one particular Monday morning, I decided to take some drawing pins from my class to assembly with me. When the children got up to say the 'Our Father' prayer, I ran around quickly and put the pins on their chairs. When they sat down, they screamed and I ran back to my seat as if it hadn't been me, but Mr Ray knew that I had done it and shouted, 'THOMPSON, GET TO MY OFFICE!'

'What for, Sir?' I asked innocently.

'YOU KNOW WHAT FOR!' he shouted and once again I was in trouble. I had to stay in the office all day and do my work there and I wasn't allowed to go out to play. I had to watch the other children playing outside from behind the window. Some of them laughed at me and I made a mental note of who they were so that I could get them back later.

One day at school, I was playing football with the boys, when a boy called Stanley kicked me so hard, I flew into a rage. I kicked him back and the next thing I knew, we were fighting. Mr Douglas, our PE teacher, tried to break us up, but I bit and kicked him too. He lifted me kicking and screaming like a wild cat and carried me all the way to the school office, where he locked me inside and left me there. I was so angry that I hadn't got to finish Stanley off that I took off my shoe and started hitting the window. I kept hitting the window until it broke, and then I took the rest of the glass out with my hands and climbed through. I ran to the playground to finish off the fight, as there was no way I was losing to Stanley. Mr Douglas could not believe his eyes when he saw me back outside in the playground. He called another teacher, Mr Mukherjee, and it took both of them using all their strength to bring me back inside. They called one of the dinner ladies, Mrs Donovan, over to sit with me in the office for the rest of the day. I did all of my work in the headmaster's office that day, but I didn't mind. I felt special being able to sit in the headmaster's office, separated from the rest of the children. I felt as if no one could trouble me while I was there because they all had to go back to class, and I had only missed playtime.

When Mr Ray heard about what had happened in his absence, he decided to send me home ten minutes earlier than everyone else for a whole week, so that I would not get into trouble with the others after school.

When I went to school the following Monday morning, my teacher, Miss Madjwick, said that I had to go to Mr Ray's office to do my work. I was happy with this idea, so off I went with a smile on my face. It felt nice to be getting special treatment, and not having to attend all the dull lessons with the other children. I felt as if going to the headmaster's office would allow us to become friends.

I began to enjoy some of my lessons. On Monday it would be English; on Tuesday, Maths; Wednesday, English again; on Thursday I would go to woodwork with Mr Douglas; and on Friday I would go to cookery class. It was just mostly the children that I didn't like as they would stare at me or look at me in a way I didn't like and then I would think, 'Right, I'm going to get you!' One day at school we were running down the stairs to go out to play when Cheryl Blackman pushed me to the floor. I screamed at her and then jumped up ready to finish her off, when the cookery teacher Maureen Bates grabbed both of my hands and held them behind my back. She shouted at me to be quiet, and as I was wriggling away from her, I pushed my head against her chest and bit her on her breast. She cried out in pain and hauled me to the school office. This, as you can probably tell, was becoming a normal occurrence for me. Mr Ray saw me in his office regularly but he still saw something good in me that no one else in my school could see. I think my mum also knew that I had more to give, but she didn't want to say anything to me, as she knew that she couldn't send me back home to Jamaica where I wanted to be.

The next day at school, Mr Ray said he needed to have a chat with me. 'Now tell me what happened to you while you were living in Jamaica, Cameta,' he asked. I began to explain how my dad had left me to go to England, followed by my mum, and then we had to move to my grandma's. I told him how Grandma had become ill and how we'd had to move again to our Aunty May's. Each time we had moved it had been a different school we had to try to fit into and make new friends. What made matters worse was that whenever I had made friends, I would later have to leave them, just like my mum and dad had left us. So, all of this had affected me when all I had needed was someone to love me and understand me, but instead, I was moving up and down and having to make new friends all the time. I told Mr Ray that leaving my friends hurt and how I had thought all the moving around was my fault. Mr Ray took the time to listen to me and made me feel as if he cared, and as if I could talk to him about anything. He understood how not being able to settle with anyone as a young child had affected me.

Mr Ray said, 'You have been through too much for someone so young, and it has made you unsettled, but now you will not go through that again. I am here to help you.'

'Cameta,' he said, 'you are a special young lady and you are going to help others one day just like yourself.'

'Thank you, Sir,' I replied, feeling much better already.

After that conversation, I behaved better and stopped fighting every day because my headmaster was helping me. I was trying to be good for Mr Ray to show him that I could do it. I wanted him to be proud of me, and when I was being good for him, I felt as if I was achieving something. Even so, I still fought once or twice. Mr Ray understood that it had all been a lot for a little girl to have gone through with very little explanation or support. He called my mum and told her that he knew I was a good person and that all I needed was love and attention from her and my family. This wasn't as easy as it sounded, as my mum had two jobs and did not have as much time for the family as we all would have liked. It was hard for her because there were so many of us to attend to as well as having to work her two jobs.

The summer holidays came, and Mr Ray called my mum and asked if he and his wife could take me on holiday with them. They had a caravan in Devon so they were going there for the break. Mum and Dad were extremely surprised that the Rays would want to take me on holiday but they agreed. I was so happy that I was going to be leaving the house for the holidays, as the only places I used to go from my house were to school, to church and the shop. This was a big opportunity for me, and I was so excited to go. I could hardly wait! This would be my first holiday in the UK and my first time away from my parents since coming to the country.

At last, the day arrived. Mr Ray and his wife picked me up from my house. Their son Adrian, who was about three years older than I, was also in the car. He was a nice boy, friendly and talkative. On the journey to Devon, Adrian and I talked loads and played I Spy in the back of the car but it wasn't long before I started to get annoyed because Adrian kept winning all the games. I decided that I didn't want to play anymore, and then he made the mistake of putting his hand on me and hitting me so I started to fight him!

Mr Ray said quietly, 'Cameta, do not spoil it. Please be good for me.'

This had the effect of calming me down so I apologised to Adrian and made more effort to be nice. It was a wonderful holiday. We went to the funfair and also to the beach where we made sandcastles. We ate fish and chips for lunch and had ice cream for dessert. It was the kind of holiday that simply allowed us to be kids. There was no chaos, just lots of fun, and by the end of it, I did not want to come back.

When school reopened after the summer holidays, I remember being well-behaved for a long time. Then one day in my English class we were all reading when a boy called Barry started teasing me, saying that I couldn't pronounce the word 'three' but said 'tree' instead. He went on and on, saying, 'You can't speak English.' I could take no more so I got out of my seat to go and beat him up. I grabbed him and shot him a box. He fell to the floor and I picked up a chair to finish him off, but thankfully the headmaster walked into the classroom and took the chair from me. Barry escaped but now I was in trouble again. I was very disappointed with myself after that and I felt as if I had let Mr Ray down.

## Fighting at Home

Life at home was mostly fun because there was always someone to talk to and someone to laugh and play with. Sometimes my siblings and I would play 'church' and impersonate the church members. However, when my dad was home, we had to be quiet; we had to play with as little noise as possible and it wasn't as enjoyable. Dad was very strict and old-fashioned and thought children should be seen and not heard.

Soon it was the summer holidays again and my mum was wondering what to do with me during this time. She knew that I would fight with my brothers at home and that we would probably mess up the house while she was at work. I got on well with both of my brothers but fighting gave us something to do when we were bored. We fought over anything and everything. My dad did not say very much when we fought. He wouldn't even ask any questions. He would just use the belt, and because of that, there were many times my mum did not tell him what was happening with us at school or home. When my dad used the belt, he used it properly! We would still feel it for days afterwards.

One day, I was fighting with my brother Wayne over a tennis ball I was trying to take from him. We ended up breaking the table in the passageway. My mum had had enough of our squabbles and told my dad. We knew that we were going to get a beating. So, when my dad came home from work, Wayne said, 'Daddy, I am ready for my beating.' My dad replied, 'Let me have my dinner first.' What both my dad and I didn't know was that Wayne had already padded himself up with books and newspaper in his clothes ready to take the beating. Once my dad had finished his dinner, Wayne asked him again, 'I'm ready, Sir, for my beating.' 'Go and fetch the belt then,' my dad replied. I remember thinking, 'Why are you asking for the beating?' I knew I was going to get one after Wayne so I didn't want him to remind my dad.

Wayne gave Dad the belt, and my dad started to lash Wayne. At the same time, he was asking, 'Why did you and Cam break the table?' and with every word, there was a lash, but Wayne was not feeling it as he was well padded. My dad realised that he was getting nowhere with Wayne that night so he gave up. I thought my brother was tough and brave. I was so happy that he had taken on my dad that night, as this now meant that I had escaped my beating. However, Wayne and I never fought again.

It was sometime later, when I was about thirteen years old and Wayne was in trouble again, that I saw him padding himself up with newspapers and extra clothes and realised that this was what he did when a beating was on the way. I realised he was not as tough as I thought he was and that this was why the beatings didn't affect him quite as much.

One incident in particular with my siblings stands out in my mind. My dad came home from work and my mum gave him his dinner. When he was finished there was still one chicken leg left on his plate. Both Jeffeth and I wanted it and started fighting over it. My mum gave me one lick so hard that I saw stars, so I gave Jeffeth the chicken leg because he was the younger one. I was not happy but I couldn't do anything about it. I felt hard done by that day.

## The Change in Me

After all our fighting, Mum decided to send me to High Wycombe for the rest of the summer holidays where my cousin Marcia lived. She was about three years older than I was – around fifteen years old. I wasn't looking forward to staying with them but once I got there, I had a good time. Marcia and I went shopping and visited her friend's house.

riday came around, she said that she was going to a young
meeting at her church. I had no choice in the matter; I
to go too. Marcia was a Christian but I was a little rebel and a
troublemaker wherever I went. However, this time was different.
I met some of her friends at the church and they were all kind to
me. The young people's choir sang and it felt good to be there.
There were loads more young people in this church than in my
church back home. The music, singing and entertainment were
bigger and better. I told my cousin that I wanted to be in a choir
just like the one at her church. 'You can,' she said.

'But I don't live down here,' I protested.

'But what about at your church in London?' she asked.

'I'm not a Christian,' I replied.

'It's not hard to be a Christian!' she laughed.

When the preacher gave the Word, he spoke about young people
and their behaviour. It sounded like it was exactly about me. I
thought that perhaps my cousin had gone and told the pastor all
about me, but she hadn't. It was the Holy Spirit. When he finished
giving his word there was an altar call. Before I knew it, I was out
of my seat and on my way to the altar, crying as I went. I asked
God to forgive me for all the trouble I had caused my parents. I
felt deeply sorry for everything wrong I'd done and felt a change
from within. While I was at the altar, a lady asked me if I wanted
to receive Christ as my personal saviour. I said I did and then she
prayed for me and told me that God had forgiven me.

All of us who had gone to the altar were asked to go round the
back of the church after the service. Someone talked with us and
prayed for us again and we were given a little book with prayers
and Bible verses in it and told to read it every day. My life
had completely changed; I felt brand new and clean. The first
Bible verse I learned was John 3:16. It said, 'For God so loved
the world that He gave His only begotten Son that whosoever
believeth in Him should not perish, but have everlasting life.'
This brought me great comfort.

Marcia had gone out for a bit so she hadn't seen when I had gone to the altar. She asked me if I had gone up and I told her that I had. 'The preacher was talking about me and I felt so guilty because the reason my mum sent me down here to you was my bad behaviour.'

'How do you feel now?' she asked.

'I feel like a brand-new person and like a heavy hat has been lifted off my head,' I told her.

'That sounds good!' she smiled.

That Sunday morning, I went back to church with Marcia. I still felt brand new and as if I was no longer carrying around a heavy load. I felt free and very happy. I wanted to jump and skip around. I could feel that something good was happening to me on the inside.

When I went back home, my mum took one look at me and knew that something was different. 'Your whole countenance has changed!' she exclaimed. 'You're glowing!'

With tears in my eyes I told her, 'Mum, that's because I'm a Christian now! I have given my life to the Lord.'
My mum was thrilled. 'Praise God, hallelujah! Thank you, Jesus! I can see the change in you!'

She hugged me and we both started to cry. We had forgotten that poor Mast Kenneth was still standing in the passageway after having dropped me home! My mum thanked him for looking after me and he said quietly, 'Prayers have been answered.' Mum agreed and we all chatted together for a while before Kenneth had to go.

That evening at dinner, my dad asked, 'Cam, how come you're so quiet?'
'No reason, Sir,' I replied.

'Hmm, you sure?'

'Yes, Sir.'

I didn't really plan on saying anything to the rest of the family as I didn't want to make a big deal about it and just thought my dad and siblings would pick it up like my mum had.

Out of respect for my dad, we always had to call him Sir or Daddy when I was growing up. My mum didn't tell my dad or the family what had happened to me that day, but they all noticed that there had been a change in me.

The following Sunday morning we had our family devotion like we always did, and when it came time to pray, I requested to go first. My siblings looked at me as if I was mad, but I just smiled. My dad said, 'Yes, go ahead,' and I prayed like never before. I cannot remember every word I said, but I remember that it went a little something like this: 'Lord Jesus, thank You for my new life, and thank You for the change You have given me. I am sorry for all I did to my parents and friends. Amen.' When I opened my eyes, my mum and dad were crying and giving God thanks for my new life. My siblings just looked at me, and Cherry, who was a Christian, asked, 'Cam, do you mean it?'

'Yes,' I replied, smiling. They were all very happy for me. Thanks be to God for that change.

From then onwards, I would pray and read the Bible and the book that the church had given to me every morning and every evening. The book was based on St John and I remember finding it very interesting. Every time I opened the book to read, I was excited to learn more.

The summer holidays were over now and it was the first Monday morning of school. Now that I had given my life to the Lord, I felt so happy to be going. When I arrived at the school gate, I saw my headmaster standing at the top of the stairs, and as I entered, he shouted out, 'Is that Thompson?'

'Yes, Sir, it is,' I replied.

He saw the change in me without my even telling him. 'Thompson, what has happened to you?' he asked.

'Sir, I am a new girl,' I responded, grinning.

'Yes, I can see that,' came his response. 'Welcome back!'

## The Change in Me at School

Many of my friends also noticed a change in me. I wasn't looking for a fight with anyone anymore. At lunchtime I decided to start a prayer meeting and my friends Monica, Andrea and Camita came along too. Camita and I have the same name but she spells hers with an 'I'. She was known as the good one and I had been the bad one for a long time, but now this was going to change. Not only did I start the prayer meeting (where Camita became a Christian), but I also took over the assemblies by teaching the school songs and reading the Bible. The teachers couldn't believe their eyes; they couldn't believe that I wasn't causing trouble and fighting anymore. I was praying and reading the Bible, and telling the children and teachers about God. Back then the attitude in schools towards Christians was very different from how it is today and Christianity was even welcomed. I invited my teachers to come to my church, and many of them came along.

I became a little missionary for God, and there was a Bible verse I would use every day. It was Psalm 121:2: 'I will lift up mine eyes unto the hills, from whence cometh my help. My help cometh from the LORD, which made heaven and earth.' The whole of this chapter was a blessing to me every time I read it.

I began to enjoy school and started to actually learn. I would do my work without any problems and would even help the other children out. When there were fights among them, I would try to stop them. What a change God had wrought within me!

I became a prefect at my school and used to help others with their behaviour. I was good at doing this because I could relate to them with all that I had been through. Although I had been through a lot, it was clear that God had had His hand on me. He was changing me for the better and giving my life purpose day by day. As time went on, things became even better for me. I settled down well and worked hard. I became the captain of the netball team and the choir leader at my school. As Camita and I were both Christians now, we used to do more things together. One thing I could never beat her at was running and she was very good at netball, too.

The time came when I turned sixteen and had to leave the school. I cried that day. I was sad to be leaving my headmaster, Mr Ray, who also cried. He cried because of how much my life had changed, and how I had gone from being a troubled, dangerous little girl to a beautiful young Christian lady going out into the big world.

Looking back on my school journey, I cannot believe how troubled and difficult I used to be, and how much I used to act up. I cannot believe how much I have changed. To this day, I still keep in contact with my friends from that school and even some of the teachers.

## College

I went to Brixton College and found it very different from Turney School. Everyone seemed so big and they were all very intelligent. My chosen subjects were Caribbean History, English, Maths, Home Economics, Typing and Social Studies. I chose those subjects because they were interesting to me, and I liked that Home Economics was about cooking. It was my aspiration to be a chef. In those days, the qualifications were not GCSE's but RSA's and CSE's.

Mr Reid was my teacher for Caribbean History. In his lessons, I learned about the Arawak Indians who had lived in Jamaica before it had been conquered by Christopher Columbus. I learned so much more about the country than I had known before. Mr Reid was a serious man and he was also Jamaican so I understood his accent. I remember that one of the first things he told the class was, 'I have passed my exams and now I am teaching you all, so it is up to you if you want to learn. I will still get my wage packet either way.'

Sometimes he would ask me to buy his cigarettes for him because he said that the rest of the pupils would not give him his change back. He trusted me and he saw some good in me.

I had a few friends there and I used to invite them to church. During lunchtime I would tell them about Jesus, and how He had saved me and that He could do the same for them. My one friend was a Caucasian girl named Kathyann. I invited her to church too. She came on many occasions but one Sunday morning happened to be a young people's meeting and the pastor's son was preaching the Word. When he had finished, he made an altar call and to my surprise, Kathyann got up and went to the altar. She gave her heart to the Lord and I was so happy that I was praising God with tears in my eyes. I shouted out, 'Praise God! Praise God! Thank you, Jesus. Thank you, Jesus.' Kathyann was the only Caucasian person in my church at that time, and by witnessing to her I had won a soul for the Lord. We both began witnessing to others and they began to come to church too and some of them even gave their lives to God. It was always such a blessing to see.

# CHAPTER THREE

# Young
## IN CHURCH

The members of my church were surprised by my transformation and so happy that I had turned into such a lovely young lady. When the time came for me to join the choir, I took the opportunity happily. It was something I had wanted to do even before I got saved because I so loved to sing. The choir consisted of about forty members and my sister Pauline was the Young People's Leader. We would sing every third Sunday, and we would go to visit other churches and perform. We had such a lot of fun doing that and I absolutely loved it.

Sometimes I would be filled with the Holy Ghost and would get into the Spirit. I remember the very first time this happened. We were singing a song called 'Jesus is the answer for the world today' and I was focusing on my own life and thinking about how Jesus had been the answer for me. I had closed my eyes and begun to cry, and as I had lifted my hands to give God praise, a feeling of warmth came over me as if someone was hugging me. I began to praise God even more, repeating the words 'Thank you, Lord' over and over again.

The other young people often looked at me strangely when I was in the Spirit as if to say, 'What is wrong with you?' At the time I did not know how to control myself, but I would sing in the Spirit and praise God. No one wanted to sit next to me in church because they knew that if I got into the Spirit I would knock off their hats if they were wearing one, as I would become lost in what I was doing!

I was a very committed Christian. I prayed a lot and read my Bible. Every day, I would tell someone about Jesus and invite them to church. When we as young people went to visit other churches, however, my sister Pauline would tell me not to get into the Spirit because it would spoil the song. Pauline didn't know that it worked like Jeremiah said, 'It is like fire shut up within my bones.' I couldn't hold it in; I had to praise Him.

Wherever I went, and whenever I sang, I would think of what God had done for me and I would find myself in the Spirit under the anointing and nobody could stop me from praising God. His hand was on my life.

There was a song that the young people would often sing and it was one of my favourites. It went like this: 'Without Him, I can do nothing, without Him I'll surely fail, without Him, my life would be hopeless but with Jesus, thank God I am saved.'

I would look forward to going to church, Bible study and the youth meetings. One day, I decided to give my very first testimony and it went a little something like this: 'Praise the Lord, praise the Lord, let the church say praise the Lord. God is good to me because He has changed my life and I couldn't have done it without Him. So, please pray for me that I will be willing to tell others about God.'

## My Jobs

After leaving Brixton College, I completed an apprenticeship as a cook at Westminster College. My first wages were £84 and I remember being so happy to receive my first pay cheque. When I told my mum how excited I was to be getting paid, she said sternly, 'Now Cam, you have to save £10 a week for yourself in case of emergencies, and I am going to put you in a pardna which is £15 a week. You must also give an offering to say thanks to

God for giving you this job. That is another £5, then £5 must go towards the shopping.' I was left with £49 to spend and I was still so happy. I used my first wages to buy a frying pan!

Sometime later I qualified as a cook, but I have worked in many different jobs over the years. I worked as a trainee dental nurse, at Gresham Road, Brixton; as a cook at Dunraven School in Streatham and as a dental nurse in Brixton with Mr Shah. I also worked as a day-care assistant at Waylands Day Centre, looking after disabled people, before taking on my final job as a health care assistant at Mayday Hospital, now known as Croydon University Hospital. I filled many different positions over the years, including a childminder position, which allowed me to stay home with Dean, my second child.

One Friday morning I got a phone call that Mr Ray, my headmaster had passed away. I was so upset. His son Adrian asked me to sing at his funeral, and I did. He was a good man. He was the one who saw good in me and he told me that I would be a good young lady and that I would help others. He was absolutely right.

Meanwhile, I continued to go to church where I thoroughly enjoyed the youth meetings because we would have a Bible quiz, testimonies and exaltation. I continued to invite people to church wherever I went, and they would often accept the invitation.

## Pregnancy

After some time, my mind began to wander, and I started to look elsewhere. My friends had begun to date and have boyfriends, which I wasn't allowed to do. Boyfriends were a complete no-no for my parents. Even so, I started to go out with my friends more often and I began to take my eyes off God. I didn't know back then that in doing so there would be danger. At the age of twenty, I was still living at home and had to ask my parents' permission to go out.

One particular day when my friends decided to go out, I asked my mum if I could go with them. She said no and that I should stay home and cook the family dinner. I was not happy. My friends were allowed to go out and have a social life but I was often not allowed to join them. I was permitted to go to church, school and to the shops but that was about it. My parents were a lot stricter than my friends' parents as they were more old-fashioned. However, on this particular occasion, I made up my mind that I was going anyway. I think my mum realised that I was still going to go when she saw that I had cooked the dinner really early. I remember her saying to me, 'Cam, if you leave this house you will not come back the same.'

I rolled my eyes and thought, 'Yeah, yeah, you've always got something to say.' I had no clue what she was on about. I was thinking to myself, 'Why should I stay and cook? I am not the only one at home!'

My mum said to me, 'You don't have to go everywhere your friends go,' and then she quoted a Bible verse to me – Ephesians 6:1 'Children obey your parents in the Lord for this is right.'

Then she said to me, 'Cam, I know that your joy is not the same anymore. What has happened?'

In a low voice, I mumbled, 'Nothing, Mum.'

I disobeyed her and went to meet some of my friends from work. At this time, I was working at a store in Clapham Junction called Arding and Hobs. I had become good friends with a few of my colleagues there, including a male co-worker who would often have lunch with me. He would also walk me to the bus stop after work if we finished work at the same time. On this particular day, my co-workers and I had agreed to meet at my male co-worker's house as we were all going to Chessington World of Adventures. However, it seemed that I was the only one on time, as he and I were alone for what felt like two hours – and during that time we got a bit too close! I'm not sure what happened to everyone else, but they turned up eventually, and we all headed off to Chessington where we all had a great time together. I didn't think too much about it at the time, but I guess looking back at it now, I was young and naive and didn't expect us to become so close when we were alone together.

When I returned home, however, my mum said to me, 'Cam, I told you that you would never be the same again.'

I wondered how she could possibly know what I had been getting up to while I had been out.

About six weeks later I began to feel sick especially when I was around food. I told my mum that I was feeling sick but she seemed to already know that I was pregnant. She told me to make an appointment to see the doctor. When I went to the appointment, I explained to the doctor how I was feeling, and he gave me a blood and a urine test. The results came back and the doctor told me and my mum that I was pregnant.

I fainted in shock! I remember sitting on the chair one minute and sometime later noticing that one of the GP's assistants was putting a cold flannel on my face, trying to get me to come around. When I eventually came around, I saw that my mum was crying. 'Cam,' she asked in a panic, 'What is Albert going to say?' (Albert is my father's name.)

And in a small voice, I replied, 'I don't know, Mum.' Doctor Reuben explained to me that I didn't have to have the baby but could have an abortion if I wanted to. I was horrified by the idea. 'I don't believe in abortion! Whatever baby I am having, I will have it because God will help me!'

Once we had left the doctor's surgery, I could tell that my mum was still extremely upset with me. 'You didn't take notice of the Bible verse I gave you, and now you are in deep trouble! What is your father going to say? That is what I am worried about.'

I turned to her and said quietly, 'Mum, don't worry. God has a plan for my life!'

I don't know how I was being calm on the outside, because on the inside I was terrified – terrified that my dad was going to kick me out of the house.

'Yes, I know, but what about the church?' she asked.

'It's not about the church. It is about me and God!' I replied. However, I felt very bad about letting my parents and the young people at the church down. Now I was going to be a mother and I was scared, but I knew that abortion was not an option for me. God would forgive me. I knew it. I had read that if you confess your sins to God, He is faithful and wants just to forgive you so I knew that He would do that for me, too.

My mum, however, was ashamed because I had been doing so well at the church before this. She called my sister Cherry and told her the news. Cherry was surprised and replied, 'You mean Cam, Holy Mary? No, it cannot be true!' Then she told my mum, 'If Dad puts her out, I will take her in.'

When we got home, Dad was in his room, recovering from a hernia operation. I told my brother Wayne about the pregnancy and he was so shocked that he punched the wall in anger and shouted, 'Dad's going to kill you!'

I went to my room and prayed. I asked God to help me to be bold enough to talk to my dad. I said, 'God you are the only one who can help in this situation. I'm sorry for what is happening. Please help my dad to remain calm.'

The next morning came and I woke up remembering that I still had to tell my dad. I made him breakfast and gave it to him, and then I gathered up the courage to say, 'Dad, can I talk to you after your breakfast?'

'Yes,' he answered.

When I went to get the tray from him, I was shaking in my boots!

I prayed again saying, 'My Jesus, You said if I asked anything in Your name You would do it. So, I leave this in Your hands.'

Because Dad was so strict, I asked Wayne and my cousin Michael to stand at the door in case he got really angry. A part of me was a tiny bit happy that he was recovering from his hernia operation, as that would mean he wouldn't be as strong to respond. However, I had back up waiting just in case. I was so scared, and so sure he was going to kick me out of the house. I went back into the room and said, 'I don't know where to start.' There were tears in my eyes, and I was shaking.

In a calm voice, he said, 'Let me start it for you.'

'But you don't know what I am going to say!' I exclaimed.

'I have an idea,' he replied, 'I know your mum had a dream that Pauline was pregnant, but it is not Pauline it is you.'

And that was when I started to cry very loudly.

'Why are you crying?' asked my dad. 'You went out and enjoyed yourself and now you come home crying!' Then my dad spoke in a parable to me and said, 'You spilt the milk on the floor, and now you have to wipe it up.' He meant that I had got myself into this mess and now I had to sort it out.

I asked him with a shaking voice, 'Do I have to leave, Sir?'

He answered, 'You have a room upstairs, so go to your room!' This made me cry even more because I didn't have to leave my house. God had answered my prayers. Thank You, Jesus! Thank You, Lord!

When I told my mum what Dad had said she smiled, 'God always makes a way when it seems there is no way. Hallelujah! Thank you, Jesus. God's hand is really on you for Albert to let you stay.' I didn't know that my mum had told Sister Daisy Thompson and

Sister Senior to pray about the situation. It is only prayer that can change people's hearts. Thank you, Lord.

After that, I had to tell the young people at church that I was pregnant. I was the first young person in the church to be faced with a situation like this. Some of them were happy for me and others were disappointed. One of the deacons in the church came to my house and told my dad that he would have to come off the church board. My dad knocked on the door and said, 'You mean this board?'

'No,' replied the deacon, 'The church board.'

'Please get out of my house, and close the door behind you!' my dad told him sternly.

The deacon also told the young people to keep away from me and my sin. When the young people told me what he had said, I felt as if I had a disease. I prayed to God and asked Him to forgive the deacon. He made it seem as if I was the only one in the world who had ever sinned. The deacon later came back to my dad and told him that he was like Eli who had allowed his sons to sin and had said nothing to them. So, my dad came off the church board. I could not believe that was my dad's reaction. God was working on him.

My dad then called me and said, 'Cam, I have forgiven you, and so has God. The only thing is that I wish you were married, but these things happen, and God will take care of you and your baby.'

The pastor of the church – Pastor Richards – came to see me. He had a different attitude to the deacon and he showed me love and compassion. We sat down in the front room together and talked. He said, 'I am sorry that this has happened to you, but God still loves you and the moment you pray and ask for forgiveness He answers you. So, don't worry, you are not on your own. I am still here for you.'

I just cried and said, 'Thank you, Pastor Richards.' He reminded me that Romans 3:23 says, 'For all have sinned and come short of the glory of God' which means that no one can condemn us. He also told me that when I had time, I should read John 4:1-26. It was about a woman who had committed adultery and who'd had five husbands but still received mercy. If God could do that for her, how much more could He do for me?

It was as if the word sex was forbidden in church. As young people, we hadn't been taught about it and yet when we got into trouble, we were told that we had to leave the church. I was the first person in my church this had happened to but I later heard of similar things happening to other young people.

Then Pastor Richard said, 'I have an envelope for you. I do not want to give it to you but it is from the principal of the church. It is a disfellowship letter. Still, remember what I told you – God still loves you!' I thanked him and took the letter and he hugged me.

Then he went and had a chat with my dad and a bit later as he was leaving the house, he told me, 'You can still come to church if you want to and you can leave before the service is over if you don't want anyone to talk to you.' He also said to me, 'Many Christians sin and hide it, but you came forward and one day this will help you to minister to other young people.'

I continued to go to church after that conversation, always making sure that I left during the closing song so that nobody could talk to me.

## Andrea Samantha Thompson

My daughter Andrea was born on the 10th of October 1979. My labour was a very, very painful one. Many times I felt like giving up and thought that I couldn't cope with it anymore, but I did and she was born safely. My mum was with me throughout the birth, and the doctor said that I had done very well for my first child. Her father, the male co-worker who I had worked with at Arding and Hobs, wasn't there. I had told him I was pregnant once I found out. He was naturally shocked but was willing to step up to his responsibilities. He was ready to meet my parents and face the music, but that was something that my dad was not going to stand for. He was very set in his ways and his word was final. He was against the idea of meeting him, and even though my mum wanted to meet him it was out of the question. My dad told me if I had anything more to do with him, I would have to pack my bags and leave. I was so grateful that he had allowed me to stay at home that I was too scared to rock the boat with him. However, I did continue to talk to the baby's father but it was in secret. I would have to go to the phone box to call him, but I dared not meet up with him.

Andrea weighed 7 pounds, 14 ounces. She was so beautiful that I couldn't stop looking at her. She had a cute button nose back then but it's now become so straight that people always comment on it. She was a very chubby baby, with a thick afro hairstyle.

Everyone at the church loved her. She was the only baby in church at that time. When I say that everyone loved her, I mean most of the young people. The older folks would give me disappointed looks as if they had never sinned before, and they were very holy. Some people thought I was showing off, but I knew that God had given me a second chance. I think some of the church members had forgotten the Bible verse in Romans 3:23 that tells us, 'For all have sinned and fall short of the glory of God.' I loved my baby and I thanked God for her! What God can do, no man can.

One Sunday morning I took Andrea to the altar and offered her to the Lord so that God would save her one day. Today, Andrea has grown to help other young girls and boys. She is a strong person who knows what she wants. She is my right hand and helps me in so many different ways. I can call on her at any time. My parents loved her very much and she was spoiled by them when she was growing up. I pray that God will continue to work in her life and that she will make a positive difference wherever she goes.

There are many young people today growing up without a father, just like Andrea did. She turned out just fine though because she had me and my whole family loving her. Andrea's life has also helped me to stop two abortions from happening. When two of my friends who had parents as old-fashioned as mine got pregnant, they came to me for advice. I encouraged them to have their babies and explained to them that they would find a way to get by. One of them had already booked her abortion appointment but after speaking with me, they both decided to keep their babies.

Back in those days, if you had a child out of wedlock it was frowned upon. Because my parents were so strict, they didn't want Andrea's father to visit my home. They did not want to meet him and my dad told me that if he came to the house, I would have to leave with him. I was disappointed and discouraged, but there was nothing I could do about it. It was my dad's house and I had to live by his rules. Andrea's father did, however, call the house and ask to speak to my parents, but my dad said no. I had to respect my dad and his house.

My parents thought that they were making things easy for me by allowing me to remain in their house, but it was hard for me to know that my baby could not know her father. I prayed to God to help me bring her up in the right way. He has never left me to this day and is always by my side. As the song says, 'I must have the Saviour with me, for I dare not walk alone. I must feel His presence near me and His arms around me thrown.' When men say no, Jesus says yes.

About five years later, around 1984, I became a Sunday school teacher and then a young people's leader. As time went on, I also became the women's president and was on the witnessing group. I was the same young girl that the church had tried and found guilty, the same girl who had been treated as if she had a disease, but God did not cut me off. He never forsook me.

If God hadn't intervened then, I would have been put out of the church at that time. Thank God, today I am still in the church, and that deacon who wanted me removed from church as if I had sinned like no other is today one of my good friends. The songwriter said, 'Jesus shall lead me all the way', and this is the reason I'm still part of His church. I continue to invite people to church and wherever I go – on the bus, at the bus stop, on the train, on the street – I tell them about God and how He loves them.

# CHAPTER FOUR

# Marriage

I met Paul at Turney School when I was about fourteen years old. I was playing rounders in the school playground with my friends when the ball went over the wall and into the schoolyard next door (Rosendale School). Being a tomboy, I climbed up on the wall to see where it had fallen. I didn't see the ball but I did see a tall, skinny boy with goofy teeth. I asked him if he had seen the ball and he said, 'You're not getting it.' I decided that I wasn't going to challenge him and just climbed back down.

I often saw Paul around but would never say anything to him. Then one Sunday he and his family came to my church. That was when I discovered that his name was Paul Junior.

Back then, we young people used to look forward to Friday nights as we had a young people's club which was so much fun. We would play games like volleyball, badminton, football and table tennis. We also had a little tuck shop where we would buy sweets and snacks.

One night, Paul turned up at youth club with his girlfriend and we all started playing badminton. He was the referee of the match and I soon realised that whenever I missed a point, he would still give it to me. I also noticed that he was smiling at me a lot. I wondered to myself, 'What's wrong with him? Why is he giving me all the points I have missed?'

I noticed that his girlfriend didn't seem very happy with him as he seemed to be paying me a lot of attention. At the end of the evening, he came over to me and said, 'You're very good at badminton.'
'Thank you,' I answered politely, even though I thought he was lying. It then dawned on me that this guy had a crush on me. I laughed to myself but it made me feel good. From that day on, he would always find something to say when he saw me, and if he couldn't say something then he would give me 'the eyes'.

My brother Wayne was the first to get married out of all the young people and he would often have all of us around his house. I remember playing monopoly there one night for hours and hours. Monopoly often caused arguments, many of which Paul was involved in. I found it funny to see him trying to get his way out of being called a cheat.

One Friday night, the young people decided to have a fancy-dress party. I went dressed in African traditional wear complete with headwrap. I spoke in the best African accent I could and told everyone my name was Miss Bimbola.

Paul went as Fidel Castro, the Prime Minister of Cuba. Dressed in his army outfit with a cap and army boots, he also had the long beard. He had turned up to the party with his girlfriend, but throughout the night he kept looking at me. At one point, I was in the kitchen cooking some fried dumplings and chicken when Paul came up to me and said, 'You're going to be my wife!'

I thought he was crazy! He had his girlfriend downstairs.

Then about three months later, my brother Wayne invited me out for his wife Lorraine's birthday. They were going out for dinner on a boat on the River Thames. When I arrived at his house, Paul and some of the other young people were there. He looked very smart. We were all dressed up, but Paul knew how to dress exceptionally well, and how to carry himself like a man. He was mature and walked with confidence. These were things I liked in a man. Once we had arrived on the Thames, I remember him coming up to me and saying, 'You look very nice.'

'Thank you,' I replied, shyly.

To which he said again, 'You're going to be my wife.'

I just laughed at him and replied, 'You're joking!'

I liked it when Paul flirted with me and I really fancied him by this time. He made me feel special, but I wasn't taking him very seriously. I knew he had a girlfriend and it made me wonder about him. I decided that the next time we spoke I was going to ask him, 'How can you flirt with me when you have a girlfriend?' A week later I went to the church youth club and when Paul came over to me, I came straight out with it. 'You have a girlfriend, so why do you keep flirting with me?'

'I'm going to break up with her,' he responded. I didn't believe him at all.

A few weeks passed and it was Paul's mother's birthday. Some of the church members had been invited to their house. I went along with my mum and some of my siblings. As I walked into the house, one of the first people I saw was Paul's girlfriend. I was surprised to see her there as he had told me they were no longer together. Shortly afterwards she called me into the kitchen and demanded, 'Leave Paul alone!' I laughed and told her that we were just friends.

I continued to attend the youth club each week, and Paul would also be there. He would be the first to come to talk to me, and would always ask how I was getting home, even though I only lived down the road. I had noticed that his girlfriend had stopped coming to the youth club, and when I asked where she was, he said that he had broken up with her. I asked him why and he replied, 'She wasn't for me. We haven't been getting on for a while.' I did not know it then but one day he would be my husband.

After some time, we began to get close and went on a few dates. We would go out for dinner, and to Jesse Dixon and Andre Crouch's gospel concerts. I started to take him a bit more seriously and started developing feelings for him over time. I would get butterflies in my stomach and feel nervous when I was around him. I could see a future with him because he and Andrea also got on very well. Andrea loved him and he treated her like she was his own child. I knew he would be a good stepfather to her, and this made me happy. He used to spend time with her and she would be the first person he would ask for when he came to the house. I felt in my heart that he was the one so I prayed about it. I asked my sister-in-law Lorraine and the mother of the church (someone who is an elder in the church and who you would go to for advice and guidance) to pray about it, as by this point, I knew I was ready to marry him. I was so happy to have someone who loved and cared for me.

As time went on, we realised that we had to tell our parents about our relationship. Paul called my mum and asked if he could come and see her. He made arrangements to meet both my parents, but before he did, he told my brother Wayne about our relationship. Wayne was happy for us. I remember him calling me and saying, 'Congratulations, Miss Cam!' I just laughed and thanked him.

Paul went to see my parents that evening and I was so nervous when he rang the bell that my heart was going boom, boom, boom. He was smartly dressed as always. I remember lying down on the floor by the door to try to hear what was being said. I couldn't hear much, but I did hear them laughing so this made me feel better. They talked for a long time and I was lying there praying that they would be happy and say yes to our relationship. He came out of the room and saw me and he looked sad.
'Did they say no?' I asked nervously.

He laughed, 'They said we have to get married because we are both in church, and we must let the pastor know about it as well.' It was around this time we decided to go on a fast with Lorraine and the mother of the church. At the end of the fast, we all shared the same scripture verse – Romans 8:28. 'And we know that all things work together for good to them that love God, to them who are the called according to His purpose.'

A few days later we went to see the pastor and informed him of our relationship. He said we would need to come and have counselling, which we agreed to, but never actually did.

Truth be told, I didn't want to have the counselling because the sessions would be from the same deacon who condemned me when I was pregnant. I was not ready to take counselling advice from him. Instead, I spoke with the mother of the church when I needed to.

A few weeks later I was out with Paul when I fell ill. I felt weak and faint, and I passed out. Paul took me to the hospital and then went to get my mum. She was not happy with this at all. She felt he was moving too fast and trying to take over. When I saw how he took care of me during this time though, it reassured me that he knew how to take care of a woman. This, along with the fact that Andrea had said, 'Mum, why don't you marry Paul, so he can be my dad?' helped me to make my decision. It was in the hospital that we decided to get engaged and set a date for the engagement party, and then we told our families and the church. The engagement party took place at my house. There was such a big turnout that people were both inside and outside the house. This was a happy time for me. I felt excited about getting married. I was in love and everyone knew so I did not have to hide it.

Paul and I went to Hatton Garden to get the ring. When I got there, I was confused because there were so many rings. How could I choose one? Paul suggested maybe picking one with my birthstone. I was happy with that and I couldn't stop smiling. Cam was in love! I came back showing off my ring. Now I felt free to hug him and hold his hand on the road.

## Getting Ready for the Wedding

It was time to start planning my wedding with both sets of parents involved. Mr and Mrs Senior came to my house to talk about the wedding preparations and how it was all going. We set a date for the 1st of March 1986. After that, we discussed who would do the catering. There were so many caterers to choose from that we were confused about who to use. We eventually all came to an agreement that the church would do the catering. So, the date was set and the catering was sorted.

We began to think about the guest list. This would prove to be a headache because I knew so many people, as did Paul. We discussed how many bridesmaids I would have, and I settled for five – my sister Sonia, my sister-in-law Lorraine, Paul's two sisters, and my chief bridesmaid, my sister Pauline. Paul chose his brother to be his best man and we had three flower girls – my daughter Andrea, Marsha Reid (the pastor's daughter) and Natasha Osborn, a family friend.

Then it was time to decide on what colour the flower girls would wear. We chose baby pink dresses, with floral head wreaths. The bridesmaids wore soft-blue dresses with white flowers in their hair. My chief bridesmaid wore a red sequinned dress and the best man, a blue suit.

We sent out three hundred invitations knowing that our church could hold six hundred people and yet on the day the church was packed. The service was held at St Matthias Gospel Tabernacle and the reception was held at Surrey Hall in Stockwell, London.

The night before the wedding I couldn't believe I was getting married. It was like a dream come true and yet I had mixed emotions. I was happy about the future but sad to leave my parents; I was also nervous, and I had diarrhoea. I'm not sure I slept a wink that night. I remember watching the hands on the clock going round.

On the morning of the wedding, I was excited that the day had finally arrived. I woke up to snow and thought I was still dreaming. Having monitored the weather for the week before the wedding I had known it was going to be cold and had been secretly hoping it would snow. A white wedding! What more could I ask for? A white wedding to match my white wedding dress! I wore a patterned, satin dress with long sleeves and five buttons down the front. I also wore a white skull cap, with a plain white veil attached, and white gloves. This was also the first time I had ever worn makeup. I wasn't fond of it because I thought it made me look completely different.

The guests wore their winter coats and boots, but it was nice to see them still making an effort. People were slipping and falling in the snow, but that didn't stop them from coming. It was a lovely wedding. One of the songs we sang was 'Love Divine' by Charles Wesley. The Bible reading was one of my favourites also, taken from Psalm 121: 'I will lift up mine eyes unto the Hills, from whence cometh my help.'

## The Reception

The reception was wonderful, too. So many people had kind things to say about us. I remember that my headmaster told Paul, 'This woman that you are marrying is not a pushover and if you give her one, she will give you two!' He meant that I was afraid of no one. Paul laughed, but it was the truth. Brother Hooker also told Paul that he should love me in the same way that God loved the church, and that we both belonged to each other and no third party should be in our life.

My mum made a mistake during the speeches and said that Paul was selfish. That did not go down very well with his family!

My pastor told us that we should make time for God and stick by His word. He also gave us a Bible verse – Psalm 91:1: 'He that dwelleth in the secret place of the most High shall abide under the shadow of the Almighty.'

During my dad's speech, he told us that we should put God first in everything and that there are no loopholes in marriage but we should never give up. He also said in Patois, 'Teeth and tongue will meet, but never go to bed not speaking to each other.'

My daughter Andrea said, 'Mum, I am glad that you got married because now I can get my Barbie dollhouse!' Bless her. Paul made sure that we not only got her the Barbie house but also Ken and his car.

Those were some of the speeches that stayed with me.

My father-in-law sang at the wedding and made everyone laugh and cry at the same time. He sang a song called 'I Went to Your Wedding' and it was so funny that people cried with laughter. I loved him deeply and he welcomed me into the family with open arms.

## Married Life

Paul and I had agreed that instead of going on a honeymoon, we would buy a house. We bought a nice little two-bedroom house in Norbury, London. Each room was beautifully co-ordinated with matching curtains, cushions and décor. We looked after our little home well. The kitchen was red, black and white and the bathroom, cream and brown with matching towels and bathroom mats. Andrea's room had Pierrot clowns on the bed linen, curtains, lampshade, bean bag, and figurines. It was a beautiful little house and I loved it. It was peaceful and calm and I really enjoyed making the house a home. Now I was going to experience what it was like to be a wife and take care of a family. I would cook the dinners, clean, iron, and do the shopping.

Six weeks after I got married, I found out that I was pregnant. We hadn't planned it but we knew we wanted children together so we were both happy. However, the happiness was short-lived when two weeks later I started having pain and bleeding. At this point, I knew I had to see a doctor. The doctor confirmed that I was having a miscarriage. This was heart-breaking for me. I didn't know how to feel. Suddenly the excitement had been whipped away and I was emotional about a baby I didn't even know. I was also scared because I was not sure if I would be able to have other children. I was confused about what had happened to make me lose the baby. It turned out that this was the first of three miscarriages. I eventually went on to have my son Dean, although a few years afterwards, I had some additional miscarriages. (I talk about these in chapter 5).

When I found out that I was pregnant with Dean, I was excited at the thought of having another chance of having a baby, but scared and fearful of the heartache I had felt from the miscarriages. I tried to remain positive and prayed to God that He would carry me through the pregnancy. I surrounded myself with positive people and made sure I took extra care of myself with the day-to-day activities like lifting and reaching for things. Paul at the time was overprotective and always tried to do things for me like carrying the shopping and doing the housework. I allowed him and others to assist me with such things and when Dean finally came into the world, I was happy and trusted God so much more. When you put your trust in God you can never go wrong. Just take Him at His word.

Before Dean's arrival, I was working for a dentist named Mr Shah who was based in Brixton. He was a lovely man who was training me to be a dental nurse. I loved the job. I met all sorts of people and I got on well with everyone. Mrs Shah would make my lunch and give it to Mr Shah to bring to work for me; that's how much they cared for me.

Mrs Shah and I had been pregnant around the same time. We had a good laugh about it and I told her it was her sandwiches that had done it! Mr Shah used to give me a lift to and from work because he lived in my direction. I enjoyed working for him as a dental nurse, and to this day he is still our family dentist.

I used to find it funny when the Caribbean customers would come to the dentist to get their gold teeth and show off with their new bling, bling. This was a trend back then. Paul also had a gold tooth and he really showed it off. There was one man who came to have his tooth taken out who was anxious because he needed four injections in one tooth. Mr Shah explained what was about to happen before he took the tooth out and the gentleman asked if he could hold my hand. I said, 'Yes, of course.' I passed all the necessary instruments to the dentist and proceeded to hold the gentleman's hand. While the procedure was being carried out, he squeezed my hand so tightly that my wedding ring dug into my skin. My fingers felt numb and turned white where the blood was no longer circulating. After he let my hand go, I saw blood coming from around the ring. I was so frightened I thought I would pass out. That was the last time I let anyone hold my hand while they were sitting in that chair!

There was also a time when another gentleman came in to have a filling done. I booked him in at reception, told him to take a seat in the waiting area and advised him that he would be next. Then I went back to the dentist's room where a patient was having a filling done and we were having to use the drill on his tooth. Once we had finished, I went back to the waiting area to call the next patient but he was nowhere to be found. A month later I saw him in Brixton and asked him what had happened. He told me that the noise from the drill had put him off so he had run out of the surgery!

Paul worked as a BT engineer during this time. He loved his job because he did shift work. Sometimes he would be on night shifts and sometimes on days. When Paul was on nights, he would call me often. He would ask me if I was all right, if I had locked the door, or if I'd had my tea yet. He would then ask if Dean was okay and ask me what I was watching on TV. Sometimes I felt like I was at work with him. I could not wait for the morning to come for him to come home.

When Paul was off work, we would go out with the children, and we would often take other children with us. We would go all over the place on our little days out, but wherever we went we always had to stop at his mum's house. He had a very good relationship with his mother. They would talk every day and he loved her dearly.

Paul would cook the dinner, do the laundry, and iron sometimes to give me a break. I always thought it was so good of him to work with me. I remember the first time he cooked: he made roast minted lamb and pork with apple sauce, roast potatoes and vegetables. We could both cook well and we both became chefs. Paul is still in the catering business doing weddings and other functions today. He was a caring and loving person who looked after me very well. He showed me a great deal of love whenever I was sick.

# Dean Robert Senior

Our son was born on 20th September 1987, weighing 9lbs. I was the smallest mum on the ward with the biggest baby! My dad and father-in-law had been debating what sex the baby was going to be. My father-in-law won since he had said from the beginning that it was going to be a boy. I wanted to include Andrea in the process and decided that whatever name she chose was what we would call him. I gave her two choices and she chose the name Dean. My father-in-law had not wanted us to call him Dean as he knew a little boy with this name who was very naughty. Still, we stuck with Andrea's choice.

However, Dean was born with eczema so bad that I could not go back to work after having him. I needed to stay home and look after him, and Paul agreed. In those days we could afford to do that, as Paul was well paid.

Dean was covered in eczema from his head to his feet. I had to visit the GP with him once a week, and many times after going to the GP we would end up in St Thomas' Hospital. I would take a case of clothes with me each time we would go to the GP in case we had to stay in the hospital because the eczema was so bad. Dean would scratch himself until he would bleed, so I had to tie socks on his hands to stop him from using his nails because this would cut and infect his skin. It was very difficult to see him in that condition. The doctors and nurses got to know me well because I was there so often.

When Dean stayed at the hospital, he would be wrapped in bandages like a mummy with only his eyes peeping out. It used to break my heart to see him this way, but I knew it was for his own good. We would usually stay in the hospital for two to three days. During one of our stays, I was privileged to meet Dr Owen, the MP, whose daughter also had eczema.

When Dean was allowed to go home, I had to bathe him and change his clothes two to three times a day. I had to keep his skin moist by smothering him with cream several times a day. His skin was all wrinkled like that of an old man, and when I changed his clothes, I would see the dead skin falling off or sticking to his clothes. He also smelt very raw. We had to change his bed linen every day as he would have bloodstains on them from the scratching. He had loads of creams and ointments which we had to use to keep his skin lubricated. One of the creams was hydrocortisone, a steroid which I had to apply to his skin carefully. Too much of it could make his skin thin, which could cause it to break and become even more sore.

One day, I was on the bus with Dean when a lady looked at him and commented, 'Eww, what's wrong with him?' She got up quickly to change her seat. I gave her a piece of my mind for being so rude and told her where to get off. When I got home, I told Paul what had happened and said I would never take Dean on the bus again. I felt hurt by the incident.

Paul and I thought about what we could do next for Dean. By this time he was about 18 months old and the creams and ointments weren't helping his condition very much. Paul's parents were living in Jamaica at the time and his sister was about to go to Jamaica on holiday. She asked if she could take Dean with her and explained that they could try some herbal treatments and see if they would help him. We agreed and she took Dean with her to Jamaica. She and her mother bathed Dean in cerasee and quarky bush several times a day. Dean spent three months in Jamaica and when he came home his skin was normal and looking good. The herbal treatments had worked. They had helped to dry up the eczema.

When he returned, I called out to him and he turned and ran away from me and back to Paul's sister. That hurt but I was glad that he looked good and was happy. Paul's sister had brought back some of the herbal bushes with her so I was able to continue to bathe him in the cerasee and quarky for some time. I thanked God that Dean did not have to scratch and hurt himself anymore. I had got my son back looking healthy.

As a mother, it is so rewarding to look at your child and see that they have learned something from you, to watch them sleep, to experience how fast they grow, to see them take on their own personality and experience something new. I'm so proud of both of my children's achievements. As a mother, I have learned to be patient, to show love and affection, and listen, even when the story being told seems long and pointless! I learned to prioritise the children's needs and to support them in all that they did.

Dean grew out of the eczema, thank God. I did a lot of praying day and night that God would change the situation and He did! Never give up praying as He hears when you call and will answer at the right time! God is never late. He is always on time. All you have to do is give unto the Lord the glory due unto his name, worship the Lord in the beauty of holiness (Psalm 29:2).

## A Change in Behaviour

Despite what we were going through with Dean's eczema condition, I noticed some signs that Paul's behaviour was changing. At first, I ignored them. I thought it was stress and decided not to say anything. After some time, however, I noticed that there was a definite change for the worse in Paul's manners and attitude. He would get angry a lot and would start swearing. I was shocked because he had always been a polite man.

There was this one summer's day when we were getting ready to go food shopping. It was around midday when Paul said that he would meet me in the car because I wasn't quite ready.

As I entered the car, I could smell alcohol on him so I asked him if he had been drinking and he said no. I told him that I could smell it on him and his reply was, 'Don't worry about me, are we going shopping or not?' We ended up arguing, but we still went shopping, barely speaking to each other.

Paul started drinking a lot; he would drink every day and it upset me. I would ask why he was drinking and suggest that we should pray. I told him that the drinking wasn't good. He would reply, 'Don't worry about it, it's not you drinking but me,' but I did worry.

I noticed on many occasions that Paul would bring alcohol in the house without my noticing until he had started drinking it. I told myself that this wasn't good but I did not know what to do so I just left him to it thinking that he would stop. However, it only got worse. He would stop at the shop and buy more drinks and the worst thing was that he would mix them. This became a habit. By then he was drinking every day and things became more difficult to manage. Paul started swearing and would often be drunk and would want to have physical fights with me. We would fight over silly things like who put the bag on the table. The drinking went on for some time.

One day I went to his mum and told her what was happening. She advised me to pray for him explaining that God could change him. Unfortunately, it continued.

One night we went out for a friend's birthday. I was looking for a pen in the car to write the birthday card out when I found more than seven little brandy bottles in the glove compartment. I was shocked! When I asked him about the bottles of brandy, he said that I should leave him alone. So, I did and I just kept hoping that one day he would stop.

We started to have real trouble when he began staying out late at night. When I would ask where he had been, he would say that he had been at his friend's house, but could not give me a person's name.

One night I had a dream. I dreamt that Paul was at a woman's house sitting on her bed. The bed linen was pink with some cushions. The woman was of slim build and dark-skinned with a lot of hair. They were kissing. In my dream, my husband was having an affair. The next morning, I told him about my dream and he laughed and said, 'You're mad. It is all in your head. When would I get the time to do that?'

I answered, 'On your days off when you go out with your friends. You always come back late at night once I've gone to bed.' He denied it, but as time went on, he continued drinking and stopped going to church. It was as if the drinking was taking over. Some time passed and I had the same dream again. I told him about it and asked, 'Why do you think I keep having this dream if it's not true?'

He replied, 'You are a witch!' and threw more abusive comments at me. I asked him to show me a picture of the woman he was seeing and to my surprise, he showed me one. Not only did he show me a picture of the woman I had been dreaming about, but it was of her in her bedroom with pink bed linen and cushions on the bed.

We had a huge argument. He claimed that she was just his friend and they weren't having an affair. I didn't believe him because things didn't add up. I realised that his days off were shared with me and the other woman. He would do what he needed to do at the house in the mornings and then would be gone for the rest of the day. He would just walk out the front door and I would not see him until that night. Sometimes he would call to ask if Dean was all right.

When he would come home, he would smell of alcohol and it made me sick. He would try to have arguments and physical fights with me and blame me for something; anything to start a quarrel. Sometimes I wouldn't answer him, but he would still go on, and then he would go back out and I wouldn't see him until the morning.

This was painful for me and the children. All I could do was keep on praying and keep it inside because I didn't want anyone to know that this was happening to me. I tried to talk to him but he was not having it. As a result, I became extremely depressed and unhappy. My mum picked up on it. She could tell that something wasn't right, and one day she called me and prayed with me over the phone. I still didn't tell her anything.

One night, Dean got sick and I couldn't contact Paul. I didn't know where he was, so I had to take Dean to the hospital in a cab. The doctors said that they would admit Dean to the hospital so I called Paul's workplace and they said that it was his day off.

I called his mum's house, but they hadn't seen or heard from him. I knew in my spirit he was with the other woman. When I got home the next morning he was there and asked where I had been. I told him what had happened and he said that he had been at work. Then I told him that I had called his workplace and they had told me that it was his day off. Still, he insisted that he had been at work in a different building.

I knew he was lying and could not believe that this was the man I had married and he was doing this to me. I could not give up at the time. I just had to keep on praying and hoping for the best. For the remainder of that week, Paul would go to work and come home on time but he was still drinking. When he was at home, he would cook which was helpful, but the following week he went back to coming home late at night.

One day Paul took Dean out for the day, and when they came back, Paul told me all about his day out with Dean and how they had been at his cousin's house. He told me that he had left one of Dean's eczema creams at his cousin's house. A few days later, by coincidence, I saw his cousin in Brixton. We stopped and talked for a while, and I told her to save Dean's cream for me that Paul had left at her house. She asked me what I was talking about and I said, 'Paul and Dean came to your house the other day, and Paul left Dean's cream there.'

She told me that they hadn't been at her house and that she hadn't seen Paul in ages. I asked her if she was sure, and told her which day it had been to see if that would jog her memory. She still insisted that no, he hadn't been to her house, and then she gave me a message to give him.

'Tell Paul, whatever house he went to, go back there and get the cream from their house because it's not at mine.' When I arrived home, I explained to Paul that I had seen his cousin and told him about the conversation we'd had. He was not happy at all. We had another argument but this time he was also upset with his cousin.

It was the end of the month and time to pay our bills, but when Paul came home, he told me that he had lost his wages. We had enough money to pay the mortgage, but not enough money for food shopping and other bills. I didn't believe his story, but what could I do? I had my thoughts that he had spent it on the other woman.

One day, I was at home when the phone rang. It was a phone call I was not prepared for or even expecting. It was the other woman. She told me her name and said that she was calling to apologise for having an affair with Paul for over a year. She explained to me that she was very sorry and asked if I could find it in my heart to forgive her. She explained that she had tried to break things off with Paul but it was hard as they worked together. She said that when she had got another boyfriend, she had ended things with Paul but he and Paul had got into a fight. She also went on to say that he had bought her jewellery (which led me to believe that's where his 'lost' wages had gone). She said that she was leaving England and emigrating to America but she felt she had to call me and ask for my forgiveness before she left. I don't know how or why but I felt sorry for her and told her that I had forgiven her. It had to have been God who touched my heart in such a way that I was able to forgive her immediately.

Shortly after this, it was our wedding anniversary. Paul took me to an Italian restaurant in Norbury. We had a delicious meal together and he proceeded to tell me all about the other woman. He told me that he was sorry, he was no longer with her and that she was leaving to go to America. He promised that it would never happen again and that he would be faithful from then on. This was a very difficult time in my life but I had to be strong in the Lord and be strong for my children. It was my faith in God that got me through this time.

The scripture that kept me going was Psalm 46. The key verses were:

**V1:** 'God is our refuge and strength, a very present help in trouble.

**V5:** 'God is in the midst of her; she shall not be moved: God shall help her, and that right early.

**V10:** 'Be still, and know that I am God.'

## A New Start

When Dean was about two years old, Paul and I decided that we needed to buy a bigger house. It was on Winterbourne Road in Thornton Heath. It was an old house which needed renovations, but it was beautiful and had three bedrooms, a good-sized bathroom with a corner bath and a lovely, huge garden. The rooms were big. I loved it and so did the children.

As I mentioned before, I couldn't go out to work because Dean had eczema very badly, from head to toe, and I needed to change his dressings and clothes three times a day. I became a registered childminder and did this work for some time. I made lots of friends with parents just by looking after their children. Some of them I am still friends with today.

I loved being a childminder, as I got to look after so many children. I would teach them to read, write, count and learn their ABC. I used to love doing arts and crafts with them and they would make things to take home to their parents. I loved taking them to the park and watching them run free. As they got older, I did cooking lessons with them and showed them how to make fairy cakes and pancakes. I also used to put on big Guy Fawkes Nights for them and they would help me make the Guy. I learnt a lot from the children, such as how they can be so different from one another, and how you have to adapt to their needs. I even learnt how to communicate with a child who didn't speak any English by making signs with her.

To my knowledge, everything was going well. Little did I know that trouble was waiting around the corner even though things seemed better with Paul and me at home. We had moved to our beautiful house and were making it our own but one day I got a call from the lawyer. He was calling to say that he was sorry that he had missed me at lunchtime when I had come into his office to sign some paperwork. I explained that I hadn't been down to his office, and didn't know what he was talking about. He said that his secretary had told him that Mr and Mrs Paul Junior had come into the office and signed some documents. I told him it hadn't been me.

He was so shocked! He said, 'Do you realise that he can go to prison for forging your signature?' I was in shock too! When I came off the phone, I didn't know what to do with myself.

Some hours passed and Paul came home. I proceeded to tell him that the lawyer had called and relayed the conversation we'd had. To my surprise, Paul swore at me and stormed off in a rage to go and get his machete. He went into the back garden and chopped down all the beautiful rose bushes, then rushed back into the house and started chopping down the bannister on the stairs. My sister Valerie, who was visiting at the time, started crying and asking Paul what was wrong with him. He told her to get out of his way before he did something he would regret.

The two children ran upstairs because they were afraid of him with the machete in his hand. I heard Andrea say to Dean, 'Let's pray because when mummy is in trouble she prays.' So, they did just that. Paul came after me with the machete and held it up to me and I said, 'In the name of Jesus, the blood of Jesus is against you,' and the machete fell out of his hand. He began to cry.

At this point, I called the kids and my sister to come and pray with Paul and me. I prayed that God would forgive him and turn his life around, because despite everything we were going through I still loved him. I later found out that the house Paul was forging my signature on fell through. Paul later explained that he had been trying to buy the house with me, but couldn't wait for me to go to the solicitors, so that is why he'd taken one of 'his ladies' along to forge my signature. He had been trying to speed up the process as he was feeling impatient.

He started coming back to church and things began to turn around. After all the prayer and fasting my mum and mother-in-law had been doing, he also started coming to Bible study and prayer meetings. I was so happy to see that prayer was working, because God said, 'Call unto me, and I will answer thee, and shew thee great and mighty things, which thou knowest not.' (Jeremiah 33:3)

# CHAPTER FIVE

# Back
## TO JAMAICA

Things had been going well for a few years for Paul and me, so we decided to build a house in Jamaica on some land that Paul had been given by his parents. We weren't in a position to sell our UK house so we re-mortgaged it instead to get some money out to put towards the house in Jamaica. Paul didn't want to rent it out because he didn't plan on our returning to the UK and didn't want the hassle of being a landlord while in Jamaica. We gave the house back to the bank.

Both Paul's and my parents had emigrated to Jamaica by this time. We used to send money to his father to buy materials for the house. We then went to Jamaica on holiday to see how the house was progressing. When I got there and saw the house it was so big – much bigger than I had anticipated, but I was happy overall. After that we went to Jamaica on holiday often to check up on the house and discussed living there one day.

It was now 1991 and the house was almost complete. Paul and I were ready to emigrate to Jamaica. My dream was coming true. I was finally returning to my home country and Paul and I would be reunited with our parents. We began shipping our belongings in a container to Jamaica. We had to send the container three months before we left the UK, so that it would be there in time for when we arrived.

In May 1991, when we were almost ready to leave, our church put a farewell event on for us so that our friends and family could come and wish us God's blessings. It was a lovely evening, but we knew we were going to miss everyone.

Pastor Harris told us that it was going to be difficult, but we must not let go of God. She said we were going to face the enemy but should never let go. She emphasised that we should stand up for God and God would be there for us. She gave us a Bible verse, which she told us to learn and repeat. Isaiah 54:17 – 'No weapon that is formed against thee shall prosper; and every tongue that shall rise against thee in judgment thou shalt condemn. This is the heritage of the servants of the Lord, and their righteousness is of me, said the Lord.'

Lots of people gave us their blessings and at the end of the evening they prayed for our family and sent us off in Jesus' name. The song that they sang was 'Take the name of Jesus with you'.

We landed in Jamaica and I could feel the heat as I stepped off the aeroplane. I felt a sense of joy overcome me as the fresh air hit my face. I was happy to finally be home. As we drove home to Mandeville in Manchester and got closer to the house, I started noticing new stores in the town. New houses were being built, the road had been extended and the area was clean.

Our house still wasn't ready so we had to stay at Paul's parents' house for a year while the workmen continued to work on the house. I didn't mind living with my in-laws. I had no problems with them; it was like it was my own house. I had a helper, Jenny, who came in and did the laundry for me and helped me to clean the house.

Paul's dad had a shop and a bar and he told Paul that he could run the grocery shop, while he ran the bar. They were next door to each other. I was concerned about Paul spending time in the bar, considering what we had gone through in London. It was not good to have Paul around a bar where he would have access to unlimited free alcohol. Paul's mum wasn't keen on Paul working so closely to the bar either. We could both see the danger it would bring. And, boy, did it bring danger our way.

## The Miscarriage in Jamaica

While we were in Jamaica, I suffered another miscarriage. God knew best so I did not question Him about it. I knew that He was in control, and what kept me going during that time was His word. Isaiah 43:2 says 'When thou passest through the waters, I will be with thee, and through the rivers, they shall not overflow thee; when thou walkest through the fire, thou shalt not be burned, neither shall the flame kindle upon thee.' Psalms 46:1 also encouraged me: 'God is our refuge and strength, a very present help in trouble.' These words kept me going during this time and I believed every one of them.

The miscarriage in Jamaica was very bad though. I was bleeding heavily so Paul took me to the hospital. When we arrived, the receptionist asked Paul for the money for me to be admitted. In our hurry to get to the hospital, we had forgotten to bring cash. I couldn't believe it. We asked if we could pay later but they weren't having it.

I was in so much pain but I had to wait while Paul went to speak to someone else. He came back twenty minutes later and told me that the receptionist had spoken to Dr Quarrie and he had said to let us in. That was what she did.

Dr Quarrie was a consultant at the hospital and also a deacon in our church. I went in and had the procedure done (a dilatation and curettage or D&C). It was a sad, fearful, confusing and distressing time. I experienced a lot of different emotions, and didn't know how to process them. All I could do was call on God and leave it in His hands as He knew why this was meant to be. Once I had gone through the procedure, I asked Paul to bring everything I needed to the hospital: sheets for the bed, pillowcases, a basin to wash in and all the usual things you need when staying in hospital. We left later but had to return to pay. At the time, we didn't have enough money to pay for the treatment because the grocery shop business was not doing well. We sold Dean's little goat and my pig to come up with the money.

I thanked God that we had been able to come up with the money. If we had not, I would have had to go to the public hospital where I would have had to share a bed with a total stranger, one of us at the top and one at the bottom.

I still felt very down about this miscarriage in Jamaica. I started wondering whether I would be able to have any more children and I thought about what would have happened if we had not been able to gather the money to pay for the treatment. It would have been such a bad experience but I had to give all praise to God who promised that He would 'restore unto me the joy of salvation; and uphold me with thy free spirit'. (Psalm 51:12)

My final pregnancy happened much later once we had moved back to England. It was a very different experience compared to the time in Jamaica. I was at work that time when I started to recognise the symptoms. I started bleeding and having cramps so I got a cab to King's College Hospital where they confirmed that I was once again losing the baby.

Going through those miscarriages helped me talk to other women who had also been through the same thing and allowed me to share my experiences with them. The most common questions women would ask me included, 'Why has this happened? Will I be able to carry a child? Why me?' I always explained to them that miscarriages are an act of nature that can happen to any woman. I would always encourage them to try again for another baby when they felt the time was right, trust in God's timing and stay positive. There have been many times when I have thought back on what I have been through, and been thankful that God's word was there to comfort me. Each time I experienced a miscarriage I would read His word and it would reassure me that God was with me.

Proverbs 3:5 stood out for me in those sad times as it says, 'Trust in the Lord with all thine heart; and lean not unto thine own understanding. In all thy ways acknowledge him, and he shall direct thy paths.' So, the Word of God became a part of my life and a great comfort to me.

Miscarriages can cause depression, loss of appetite, isolation and strain on the marriage relationship. This is what happened to me. I found it difficult to explain how I felt after each miscarriage and felt guilty as if it was my fault that our family wasn't expanding. Miscarriages also bring about fear but we know that God has not given us the spirit of fear, but of power, and of love, and of a sound mind (2 Timothy 1:7). God does not want us to live in fear. You can always try again which is what I did after the first three miscarriages after which God gave me our baby boy, Dean.

## Paul's Grocery Shop

Living in Jamaica, Paul would stay in the shop late each night, drinking with his friends, and they would play dominoes until all hours. Sometimes, his dad would play with them. Almost every Friday night there would be a fight, and they would send for me to stop the fights. Out of respect, the people in the community called me 'Miss Cam'. Almost every Friday night someone would say, 'Run guh fi Miss Cam.'

There were some workmen building houses in the area and they asked if I could cook some food and sell it to them. This led to a contract with them. I would get up early in the mornings to cook their lunchtime meals. I had to have them ready by noon. Paul and I were doing well financially at this time with him in the grocery shop and me with my cooking business. I enjoyed it but it was hard work.

I attended the church down the road from where we lived and would always know if I was running late because I could hear them singing from the house. This was my mother-in-law's church where she was in the church choir. She would sing and read her Bible every day. Everything about church in Jamaica was completely different from church in the UK. The church building was different. People outside could look through the open windows and see what was going on inside the church. The children were dressed smartly and the girls wore a lot of colourful bobbles in their hair. The ladies all wore hats and you could tell that everyone took pride in their appearance on a Sunday. They took church seriously and gave meaning to the phrase 'Sunday best'. This reminded me of when I was a child and had gone to church. Everyone seemed happy to be there.

My father-in-law got saved at this church. He was never late for church either. He would get dressed and just leave us behind if we were not ready. He loved the church and he loved singing. He was a happy man who could always make us laugh. He would sing some old-time songs I had never heard of and then ask, 'What! You never heard those songs?'

I loved the church and the people were friendly and kind. I used to enjoy Sunday mornings when the choir would sing and they would look beautiful in their uniforms. I used to like seeing the children coming to church also. They looked so festive with their pretty dresses, colourful beads and ribbons in their hair. Church was always a good time for me.

Paul and I had been married for five years at this point. Sometimes he would come to the church with us. However, from time-to-time, problems would arise between us. One Saturday night when we had run out of sugar at the house, my mother-in-law asked me to go and get some from our shop. I went to the back entrance of the shop, which was located by our garden. As I got to the back door, I could hear talking, so I looked through the hole in the iron door – the part where you would push your hand through to put the padlock on – and I saw Paul with a female. She was against the wall, and Paul was standing in front of her, really close. He had one hand on the wall just over her shoulder, and a glass in the other hand (he was drinking alcohol). I opened the door and asked her what she was doing at the back of the shop which was only for staff, and she replied that my father-in-law had let her in.

Paul told me to leave her alone, and I replied, 'No, she needs to get out.' Then I went to get the sugar but I told her that before I returned, she'd better be gone.

I calmly returned to the house with the sugar before heading straight back to the shop to have it out with her but when I got back, she wasn't there. Paul and I started to argue about it. He followed me out of the back of the shop and grabbed me from behind and we started fighting. We were wrestling with each other and I could feel that I was about to fall over into the gully where we used to tie up the cow. I decided that I wasn't going over there on my own, and held onto Paul as we both fell, rolling down the gully – and then I heard a voice.

'Is that Sister Senior fighting?'

When I looked up, I saw the pastor. I got such a fright and so did he.

There are many more stories I could tell of the turbulent time in Jamaica but I won't go into any more detail as I would like to share some of the good times. After this incident, I decided that I needed a break, left Jamaica and returned to England. First though, let me rewind a bit and tell you about some of the good times I had while living in Jamaica as an adult.

I loved living in Jamaica. I would always be looking to see where I could help others. First, I began helping the elderly (known as the shut-ins). These were people who were unable to leave their houses. I would bring them groceries and pray with them. I also began to help children who couldn't afford to go to school by paying their school fees and giving them food to eat. I became well known in the community and people would often come to me for help and advice when they were facing difficult times.

## Back to England

I came back to England on my own for a break from all the problems at home. I lived at Sister Richard's house. She was the mother of the church. I got a job as an assistant cook at Dulwich

Hospital. About two months later, Paul came to England with Dean. We had lived in Jamaica for almost four years but now we were living apart back in England. Paul and Dean were living with Paul's sisters in South Norwood. It was a difficult time for me as I had originally left Jamaica to get a break from Paul and the stress we were going through. It was difficult as Dean would want to see me and stay with me, but I couldn't keep him as I had to go to work and he wasn't in school yet.

After some time, my friend Audrey Thompson heard that I was back in the UK and she came to visit me. She said that I could come and live at her house. I quickly said yes and took up the offer. By this time Paul and I were trying to make things work so Dean, Paul and I all moved into Audrey's house and we lived there for some time before sending for Andrea. At the time, Andrea was living in Jamaica with my parents and was in a high school there.

Years later, my sister-in-law and I were in Jamaica on holiday when my father-in-law became ill with Alzheimer's. He needed someone to look after him. We noticed that something was a little off when he would say things that didn't make sense, repeat himself often, and sometimes push people away. He got upset over the simplest of things and would say that he hadn't eaten all day, when he had in fact eaten breakfast, lunch and dinner.

As his condition became worse, he spent a lot of time talking about his childhood days and asking us questions as if we would know about his childhood. We started asking around for a male carer and my mother-in-law's sister suggested a young Christian man that she knew. She said he didn't keep too many friends and might be good for the job. We went to look for him, but could not find him. I asked a cousin of the family to find him and bring him to my mother-in-law's house.

One afternoon the cousin turned up at the house with three men. As she was coming towards me, my spirit told me that it was the one in the middle. When he smiled, I thought, 'Yes, that's the one,' but my mother-in-law and sister-in-law said that he was too small to help my father-in-law. I said, 'Give him a try,' but my mother-in-law felt that he wouldn't be able to manage my father-in-law should he ever have a fall. 'He will manage,' I asserted, 'and to be sure you can give him a trial.' So, they did and he exceeded their expectations and got the job. His name was Eddie Goss.

Shortly after this I returned to England, and each time I called Jamaica my mother-in-law would tell me how well Eddie was doing with my father-in-law and how they had warmed to each other.

Each time we would go to Jamaica on holiday, Eddie would come and pick us up from the airport. He also became our taxi man who would take us around. Eddie became a very good friend to the family. One of the times Eddie came to collect us from the airport, he borrowed a white van as there were a lot of us and a lot of luggage. He packed all the luggage into the white van and we all got in. Eddie then went to close the door but to my surprise it fell off in his hand. We could not stop laughing but he was able to put it back on, and get us home.

At the end of that trip when he was seeing us off at the airport he said, 'I will come to England one day!' and I replied with, 'Yes, and you'll be coming to my church!' This has now come to pass and to this day Eddie is still my taxi driver.

Paul and I decided to look for a place of our own, although living with Mr and Mrs Thompson had been a blessing for us. They treated us very well and I am still best friends with them to this day. Paul and I signed up to the council and housing trust because we no longer owned a house in the UK. The housing trust gave us a property very quickly because Paul was sick at the time with sarcoidosis.

When we were called to look at the house, Paul and I both went but Paul went ahead of me and reached there first. I rang the bell when I arrived and he opened the door. I felt at peace as I went in, even though I didn't look all around. I knew that this was the one. It was a three-bedroom with a lovely garden.

Paul got better and went back to work after recovering and learning to live with sarcoidosis and I got a job right next door in Croydon University Hospital, which was called Mayday Hospital at the time. I worked there as a health care assistant. After five years, Paul and I bought the house and I am still living there to this day.

The house was a blessing from God and became a refuge for helping others such as families and friends. The people who came in felt peace, love and plenty of joy. Most of the time, people didn't want to leave. I would often have dinner parties, prayer meetings and social gatherings there. Those who came for a week ended up staying two weeks, and those who came for a month stayed several months. I like to believe it was down to the love and peace that was shown. People also came from abroad and stayed with me.

After some time, trouble started again between Paul and me. Paul had promised that he wouldn't give me any more trouble but unfortunately this promise didn't last. I decided that I was not going down that road again because it hurt too much. Paul started to drink and cheat on me again. I kept on my knees and read the Bible. Paul showed that he didn't care. Sometimes when he would go out, I wouldn't see him until morning, and this went on for some time. He would abuse me mentally. I tried to get help for him but he didn't want it. He would just carry on as if I wasn't there. So, I called his pastor and my pastor because we went to separate churches. I had written down everything he was doing and showed it to the two pastors. They asked Paul if everything I had written down was true and he said, 'Yes.'

The pastors talked and prayed with us, hoping there would be change, but the problems continued. It was as though everything the pastors had said to us had gone in one ear and out the other. We were now living in the house separately. It was very uncomfortable, but I never stopped talking to him. I would say, 'Good morning,' if I saw him, but he wouldn't answer. I would go into my room and cry and just talk to God to change him but it was like God was not answering my prayers, so I went on fasting until I got an answer from God. It came as soon as I had finished praying and I opened the Bible. It was Psalm 16:1 and it read in capital letters 'PRESERVE me, O God, for in Thee do I put my trust.'

Then my prayer partner called and gave me this Bible verse: Psalm 18:16 and 17 – 'He sent from above, he took me, he drew me out of many waters. He delivered me from my strong enemy, and from them which hated me; for they were too strong for me.' All I could do was give God the praise because He knew my future. I continued to fast and pray for three days. Another of my prayer partners called and gave me the scripture the Lord had given her. It was Psalms chapter 20. I found some key verses in it. One of them read, 'The Lord hear thee in the day of trouble; the name of the God of Jacob defend thee.'

Then I said to myself, 'God is making a way for me.' I only had the Word to hold onto. At this time, I didn't know that more trouble was coming my way.

The last word I got, at the end of the fasting period was, 'FOR THE BATTLE IS NOT YOURS BUT THE LORD'S' (Chronicles 20:5).

After that, Paul decided to leave home for a few days. He didn't say he was going. I just noticed that I hadn't seen him come or go for about three days. When he returned home, I was sitting in the dining room and I heard him come in. He went into the front room as he was using it as his bedroom at the time. I assume he went to put his stuff down before coming to speak to me. He knocked on the dining room door and opened it and then he asked if he could speak to me and I said, 'Yes.'

He stood in the doorway and said, 'I'm looking for somewhere to go.' He said it was best that he went as things were getting worse, not better.

'Okay,' I replied with a heavy heart. Part of me wanted him to go and another part couldn't believe this was happening. I was devastated and shocked, but little did he know that I already knew that he was going out with one of the girls in his church. I had followed Paul one evening in a cab to see where he was going. He ended up in Tooting and I recognised the girl who opened the door. We had been in a store in Tooting in the past when he had been talking to the same girl, but he hadn't introduced me to her. Shortly after this, his friend Michael had been getting married in Jamaica and Paul had gone to the wedding with some of his friends as well as the same girl from Tooting. I had been notified by numerous people that he had taken a girlfriend with him to Jamaica. On his return, I had told him I knew of his girlfriend that he had taken to Jamaica. He denied it.

Sometime after this, there was a concert taking place at Marsham Street in London. I went along with my sisters. When we arrived at the meeting place, we exited the car only to see the same girl sitting in a car, waiting. I walked right over to her and opened the door. We exchanged some words through which she angered me and I proceeded to slap her. I told her to get out of the car but she wouldn't and she held on tightly to the steering wheel. I dragged her out of the car and started hitting her. I remember one of the church members saying, 'No, sister Cameta, don't hit her!' but a quiet voice whispered to me, 'Lick her!'

My sisters and a few of the church members came to stop me and broke it up. We had all made our own way to the concert. At the end of the night, I had seen her go up to the altar for prayer and I don't know why but I felt sorry for her.

On my way out of the building, she saw me coming and as I got closer, I noticed that she had a bottle of perfume in her hand. She turned to me and said, 'Here, you can have this, I don't want it anymore.' She threw the bottle of perfume at me!

I kicked off my shoes and chased her down the road. When I got a hold of her, I gave her some licks until again we were broken up by the others.

About a month later she sent me a letter of apology, explaining what had happened, and admitting that all that I had heard and seen was true. She confessed how sorry she was.

Remember, all this time Paul was still living in the same house, although we were living separately.

So, here's a message for the Christian ladies who may be dating a married man. It is totally wrong. It never works out for the good of anyone who comes in between a marriage. It ruins families and you are only setting yourself up to fail by doing this. If a man is willing to cheat on his wife with you, he will also cheat on you. The Bible says, 'Therefore, what God has joined together, let not man put asunder.'

The Bible also says, 'And I say to you, whoever divorces his wife, except for sexual immorality, and marries another, commits adultery; and whoever marries her who is divorced commits adultery.' (Matthew 19:9)

# CHAPTER SIX

# Weathering
## THE STORMS

### First Mini Stroke

One Saturday morning in 2005, I woke up to go to the bathroom and found that I couldn't stand up. I kept falling over. I tried to get up a few times but couldn't. I didn't understand what was going on or what was wrong with me. I had been fine the night before. I hadn't been particularly ill either and had only experienced a few headaches recently. At this point, I was frightened, nervous and confused.

Having worked in the healthcare profession the thought crossed my mind that it could be a stroke, but I didn't want to believe it. At the time, Paul and I were not on good terms, but I called him anyway and he came into the bathroom and saw me on the floor. He said, 'You need to go see the doctor,' and picked me up and helped me get ready for the GP. When we went in to see the doctor, I explained what had happened and how I felt. The doctor said, 'I think you are having a stroke,' then wrote a letter for me to take to the hospital. When I arrived at the hospital, I began to feel lightheaded and dizzy. The nurse took my blood pressure and said it was very high. I tried to talk, but it seemed as if I was talking like a little girl. That was when I knew for sure that something was wrong with me. I didn't want to think the worst though so I still wouldn't believe it until I was told that it definitely was a stroke.

I knew all the signs but didn't want to accept it. This couldn't be happening to me – a stroke – surely not!

The doctor carried out some tests and by the time they were done, I couldn't speak very well and had become very weak. My right arm and leg had become paralysed. I had now become a patient instead of a nurse, and all in a matter of hours. I was given a lumbar puncture which entailed a needle being inserted into my back and some spinal fluid being withdrawn. It was very painful and left me with a bad headache.

The porters would come each morning to collect me for my physiotherapy session, but one morning a porter I recognised came along. It was my nephew Neil, who was working at the hospital at the time. He said, 'I've come for you.' I told him that I could walk but when I tried, I fell over and he laughed and then helped me up. I simply did not want to go in the wheelchair. There were times when I would cry because I could not help myself. It was very difficult and frustrating for me, but I thanked God that my family was there for me.

A few of the doctors who knew me very well would come during their lunch breaks to help me walk. I stayed in hospital for four weeks. I was told that the stroke had been caused by a little blood vessel that had burst inside my head. This was all to do with stress and high blood pressure. The doctor explained that when you go through difficult times, you need to talk about them to relieve the stress. I had kept my troubles bottled up inside and this was the result. I'd had a stroke.

I prayed that God wouldn't pass me by. The scripture that came to my mind was 1 Peter 5:7: 'Cast your cares upon Him, for He cares for you.' I believed every word as it could only be God who could get me through this. This experience taught me to voice how I am feeling, and to try not to bottle things up. I know this is easier said than done; however, our health is precious to us so it is worth it. Stress causes a lot of illnesses that can lead to serious life-threatening situations.

Throughout my time in hospital, and given that I lived just next door, Paul would pop in to visit me. One day, he brought a girl with him to see me, but he did not know that I had seen her before. This was the girl he was cheating on me with and she did not know that I knew. As soon as I saw her, I tried to tell Paul to take her out but he did not understand what I was saying and was wondering why I was so upset. She gave me a present – some bubble bath. I told Paul to take it and wash himself with it and that he should get out of my way. I did not want to see either of them again.

After a while, Paul realised that I knew who she was and I did not see him again for about two days. When he came back to see me, he tried to justify himself but I just told him that I knew her. It was very hard to explain to him because I was still struggling with my speech and it took me a long time to get the words out. He was very surprised and I could not believe that he could do something like that to me while I was unwell in the hospital. My blood pressure went up and Paul had to leave. I was absolutely fuming! I was so angry that if I'd had the strength, I would have punched them both. They had tried to make out that she was Paul's good friend but mama didn't raise no fool! He had hurt my feelings and my pride, and humiliated me all at once in front of my friends who had come to visit me. It was obvious what was going on between them and even my friend was angry about it when she saw them turn up together.

One night while I was still in the hospital, my condition deteriorated and the doctor tried to locate Paul. They could not find him even though they kept calling him. They called his workplace too but were told that it was his day off. The next morning, he came to the hospital and when the doctors told him that they had been trying to reach him he said that he had been working. Of course, we all knew that he was lying because of what his workplace had said. It was clear that he hadn't been working but had been with his girlfriend that night.

The time came when I was ready to leave the hospital. I was worried about whether Paul was going to take care of me but he did with the children's help. It was very difficult for me even to comb my hair, brush my teeth and put on my clothes, but thankfully with the help of my two children and Paul, I got by. All that was keeping me going during that time was the Word of God in my mind telling me that the joy of the Lord is my strength and to God be the glory.

I began to recover slowly. First, I began eating and then I started using my hand. After that, I started trying to walk. I had good and bad days. On a good day, I would go downstairs and try to interact with the family and any visitors. I would exercise my hand and leg. On a bad day, I didn't want to talk or do anything; I would just stay in my bed and reflect on my life and how I had gotten to this stage. I would try and pray to keep myself going, and even when I wasn't up to it my church family would come to visit, pray, sing and encourage me, and remind me of who I was: a woman of God. This is what helped me through it all.

## The Safety Pin

After I had recovered from the stroke, things between Paul and I calmed down and we functioned more like a normal family. We all went to Jamaica for a holiday and had a great time. On the day that we were due to fly back to London, we were getting ready to leave. I bent down to pick up my hand luggage and felt a sharp pain in my lower back, just above my waistline. I cried out and fell to the floor, and then I couldn't get back up.

My daughter came rushing into the room and asked, 'Mum, what happened?'

'I don't know,' I replied.

The taxi came to the house to pick us up for the airport but I was in too much pain to go, so Paul and my son flew back to London while Andrea stayed with me in Jamaica. Eddie took me and Andrea to the GP but when we got there it was difficult for me to get out of the car because of the pain. We eventually managed to get into the doctor's surgery and had to pay a fee before the doctor could see me. When they called me in, I had to undergo blood tests and have some x-rays taken. After taking four x-rays the nurse called me into the clinic and said that they needed to take three more because they were not happy with the ones they had taken. She explained that what they were seeing wasn't making any sense. I was concerned and I started to worry, but Eddie told me, 'Don't worry. Just pray. God has it all in control.'

While waiting for the doctor to call me again I was thinking about what could be wrong. After some time, the doctor called me in to see him, and Andrea and I went in. The doctor said, 'I don't know what to say to you, but we found a safety pin in your spine! So may we do two more x-rays without your clothes on to make sure there are no pins on the hospital gown?'

So, they took two more x-rays and they still showed the safety pin in my spine. I could not understand it. Andrea, Eddie and I were baffled and lost for words. The doctor said, 'Let me ask you this silly question: did you perhaps swallow a pin or did you eat one in any food?'

I answered, 'No, I am a big woman. Why would I want to do that?'

He said, puzzled, 'That's what I would like to know.' The doctor said that the good thing about it was that the pin was closed. Thank God, because otherwise, it would have caused more damage. He could not do anything more for me and told me, 'All you can do is hope to pass it out. Come back and see me in three days.'

I was amazed, shocked and afraid. I wondered how it had got there. I was afraid of the pain it was causing. The pain was so bad that I was walking bent right over like an elderly person. I was afraid it might also cause more damage and scared that it might open.

When I went back to the doctor's room, I had to have two more x-rays taken. The pin was still there. I went home and started to pray even more. I also sent a message to London to ask the church to pray for me. Paul called and told me that he believed that someone had put the pin in my food and I had eaten it without noticing it. This was the only explanation he could come up with, but it just didn't make any sense as to how it was in my body. How could it get from my stomach to my spine?

I replied, 'Listen to me. No weapon that is formed against me shall prosper (Isaiah 54:17). I am God's servant and He told me to cast all my cares on Him and that is what I am doing.'

I spent two more weeks in Jamaica before we travelled back to the UK in first class seats. It was the first time Andrea and I had travelled first class. I had a seat that turned into a bed so I had lots of room. I felt very important because I was called by my surname, 'Mrs Senior'. We had newspapers to read and were given a good portion of food on proper plates, with proper cutlery. The medical team was waiting for me when I disembarked, but thanks be to God I could walk even if it was with a limp.

When I came home, I made an appointment to see the GP and they gave me a letter to take with me to the hospital. When I went to the appointment the doctor looked at my x-ray and was amazed. 'I don't understand this. You are still walking well.'

They sent me for yet another x-ray, and this time the pin had moved from my spine to outside my spine so the doctor said they would just keep an eye on it. I never gave up. I just kept on trusting God and believing that He would supply all of my needs and God did it all for me. I did not have any operations. All the doctor did was keep an eye on it because the pin was moving. I had overcome in Jesus' name and my x-ray proved it. Up until this day they haven't been able to say how the pin got there or what happened to it, but it somehow disappeared.

## The Asthma Attacks

One Wednesday night in early 2007, we were having a prayer meeting. The gas heating was turned on because it was cold. I started coughing and couldn't stop. I was struggling to breathe and my chest was so tight it felt as if someone was strangling me.

I was gasping for air and it sounded so bad. I realised that I was having an asthma attack. I had never had one before. As I was struggling to breathe, I was thinking, 'Why isn't someone calling an ambulance?'

Instead, they started to pray for me at the top of their voices but then Sister Beverly realised that it was an asthma attack and she took me to the hospital. I was admitted for three days where they put me on oxygen and a nebuliser. That was the first of two asthma attacks.

Later that year, on a Monday morning, I woke up, had my devotion time and headed downstairs to make my breakfast. My slippers were at the bottom of the stairs but as I was pushing my feet in, I realised that they simply wouldn't go on. When I looked down, I realised why. There was a mouse in one of my slippers! I cried out loudly and tried to run back up the stairs, but I fell three times in fear. I really don't like mice! I eventually managed to get up the stairs. My daughter came round to the house around the same time as I reached the top of the staircase. She rang the bell but I talked to her through an upstairs window and told her that there was a mouse in the passage. She didn't understand what I was trying to say and when she opened the door she ran back out again and called my neighbour who came and killed it. The ordeal was so much for me that I ended up in the hospital again with another asthma attack. Can you imagine that I ended up in the hospital because of a mouse? To this day mice don't like me and I definitely don't like them!

## Second Mini Stroke

My mother and father-in-law had come to visit us in London. When it was time for them to go back to Jamaica, Paul and I went to collect them to take them to the airport. When we arrived at Paul's sister's house, I was going up the stairs when I felt as if someone had hit me on the head. I became very dizzy and was seeing double but I didn't tell anyone. I went to the airport just the same and on the way back I told Paul how I was feeling.

Paul took me to the doctor and he told me that I was having a mini stroke. I was then taken to the hospital and kept in for about two weeks. The scan showed that I'd had a bleed on the brain. The stroke affected my right hand, my speech, and my right leg. As time went on, I tried to remember the Word of God that said, 'The Lord is my shepherd; I shall not want.' (Psalm 23:1.) God really was my shepherd. He was looking after me in those sad days. The Word said that He would not leave me nor forsake me and I believed it. This was my second out of three mini strokes.

## The Separation

Paul and I had been living separately in the same house for over a year. During this time, I believe God was preparing me for what was about to happen. The time came in November 2008. He asked me if I wanted a cup of tea and I answered, 'Yes.' He made the tea, and then came and sat down and began to take his house key off his bunch of keys. Then he gave it to me. We both started to cry and he hugged me, saying, 'I gave you too much trouble, so it is best if I go.' I cried as he closed the door behind him.

As the days went on, I started to feel a sense of freedom. I was no longer waiting to hear him push his key through the door. I used to be able to tell his mood by the way he opened the door and I would become anxious if I knew he was upset. It felt more peaceful now because I wasn't tensed up and expecting to have any disagreements. I was free in my home. I got my front room back, and my space where I could watch people going by through the window. I also felt a sense of freedom for my children. Dean was somewhat relieved from the stress of seeing his parents living under the same roof but not together. Andrea could come and go as she pleased as she didn't live with us but had felt awkward when Paul was around because she could always feel the tension.

About a month later, I was in the dining room when the doorbell rang and to my surprise, Paul was at my door. He came in and proceeded to ask how I was doing. All along I was thinking, 'Just get to the point.'

He then asked if I would take him back.

'Will you change?' I asked him.

He replied that he had nothing to change, to which I responded, 'If you're not going to change then you cannot come back here.'

'Okay then, look after yourself!' he replied and walked out.

That was the last time I saw him in my home.

## Breast Cancer

Once I had been discharged from the hospital, I went to stay at my daughter's house so that I could recover from the stroke. While I was there, I thought, 'Let me examine my breasts,' and to my surprise, I found a little lump in my left breast; I knew exactly what it was. I did not say anything to anyone and after two weeks had passed, I examined myself again and discovered that it had become a bit bigger. Still, I said nothing. About six weeks later I examined myself once again and by now it was the size of a grape. I was still off work sick, but that morning I decided that I was going to see the doctors at the hospital I worked at.

The doctor examined me and sent me for a mammogram. A few days later they called me to tell me that they needed to do some biopsies. They did thirteen biopsies on me and the following Monday morning I received a phone call telling me that I needed to come to the clinic on Thursday afternoon. I knew straight away what it was because they had called me back so quickly.

At this time, Paul and I were not on good terms and he wasn't staying at the house. I asked my two children to come with me and asked them if I should tell Paul. One of them said that I should tell him and the other said not to. In the end, I told him and he came to the appointment with me and the children. I told them all to expect bad news because the hospital had called me back so quickly. We arrived at the hospital for my appointment and I was called in to see the doctor. I knew the doctor personally as I had sometimes worked with her in her clinic. That day, the doctor's face was red like a cherry and the nurse looked sad but I was not afraid because I knew what they were going to say.

The doctor began. 'Hi, Cameta, how are you?'

I answered bravely, 'I am good and not afraid.'
Then she said, 'I don't know how to tell you this but you have stage 3 cancer and I am very sorry. You will need chemotherapy and radiotherapy.' She then explained my options and how we could proceed. She explained that they would remove the cancer by performing an operation and asked me if I had any questions. All I remember saying was, 'I will go through this with God.'

'Cameta, you have a strong faith,' she replied.

On the way out of the hospital, Paul turned to me and asked, 'Are you going to be all right?'

'Yes, I have my family and the Lord with me,' I replied.

After two weeks, I received another call from the hospital saying that I needed to come in to see the doctor. When I arrived, a registrar doctor saw me and told me that he was going to do the operation. When I asked him some questions, he didn't give me very good answers. My daughter asked him a question too and he was rude and simply ignored her. I told him he was not going to touch me.

He replied with, 'I am the consultant and it's my job to remove your breast.'

'You won't be taking off my breast!' I replied. 'I am a staff member and a patient, and this is how you want to treat me?' With that, I walked out of the clinic. I was so angry that I reported him.

The hospital called me twice within a two-day period to tell me about cancellation appointments so that I could schedule the operation. Each time they called, I asked them who would be doing the procedure and when they said it would be the same male doctor, I told them, 'No thanks. I will not be having it done by him.'

I asked for the lady doctor and they said that she was on holiday for two weeks. I asked if I would die in two weeks and the person on the telephone laughed and answered, no. I told them I would wait until she was back then, and two weeks later the female doctor called me and said that she was going to do my operation. I was happy. She did my operation and it all went well. The operation was a lumpectomy which means that she was able to remove the lump without removing my whole breast. I was very happy with the end result. She did such a good job and today I have both of my breasts. One is bigger than the other, but I am not complaining!

Thanks be to God. Three weeks later, I started my treatment at the Royal Marsden Hospital in Sutton.

## Treatment

On 17 August 2009, I had my first chemotherapy session. Chemotherapy was a whole day affair. I would arrive at the hospital in the morning to have a blood test and wait to see the consultant. After my appointment with the consultant, I would have lunch, and then I would be given a buzzer. When the buzzer went off it meant I was ready to have my chemotherapy session. I would have to sit down while the medicine entered my arm through a drip. This would take around an hour and twenty minutes to be completed. The nurses would come to remove the cannula from my arm and I would have to wait for another ten or twenty minutes before I could leave. The chemo would leave me feeling very sick, dizzy and nauseous.

Paul took me to my first chemotherapy session, and on the way back home he said, 'I would like to ask you a question.'
And I said, 'Yes.'
Then he said, 'But you don't know what I am going to ask you.'

'Yes. I know and you can have it.'

And he said, 'But you are going to think that I am wicked.'

So, I said, 'Yes, you are wicked but you can have the divorce.'

Paul was surprised that I had known what he had been going to say.

I told him, 'I have two types of cancer, and one is a bad one.'

'I thought it was only one type of cancer,' he exclaimed, surprised.

I replied, 'You are the bad one, so you have to go.'

Soon after that conversation, I received a letter from Paul's solicitor stating that he wanted a divorce. The first letter that came said that the marriage had broken down because of a lack of communication. I did not sign it because it was a lie. Then the second letter came, reading that we had been separated for some time and I still did not sign it. Finally, I got another letter. He had agreed to say that adultery was the reason the marriage had broken down. I signed that letter.

The divorce proceedings began and I started thinking about how I was going to manage on my own and how I was going to pay the bills because Paul had done all of those things in the past. He knew where to go to pay the bills and other things. After some time, Paul and I started having mediation sessions where we would meet once a week to see if anything could be resolved and to make a decision about what to do with our property in Jamaica. Each time we met, we became upset with each other and would go back and forth. The lady who spoke to us was pleasant to us and was a Christian as well. I don't know if Paul knew but I did.

Each time we met, I would get upset about what was happening to us but Paul had already made up his mind as he was now going out with another girl from his church. He told me that he didn't have anyone but he did. We had many meetings and it got to the point where the meetings were getting hard for me because they were bringing up the past. I found it very painful. We concluded that the house should be sold and I would get my half of the proceeds. The divorce caused problems between Paul's family and me. When I got married, I saw it as though I had gained a second family, now suddenly things had changed. It was like a bereavement where one minute a person is there and the next, they're gone. Thankfully, there has been reconciliation between some members of Paul's family and me but it just goes to show what divorce can do and how it can separate families. Thank God that He is always there.

Sometimes, we have to forget those things that are behind us and reach forward for those things which are in front of us (Philippians 3:13-14). I had to pray to God to help me go through this because it was extremely painful. It has taken me years to get over it and I know it was only God Who helped me.

Meanwhile, I continued to have chemotherapy and radiotherapy, and with that came several side-effects. I lost my hair. I lost my toenails. I lost my eyebrows. I had ulcers in my mouth, under my arm and my foot. I had diarrhoea and vomiting. I lost my appetite. I experienced sleepless nights. I hated the nights so much I couldn't wait to see the morning. The chemotherapy happened every two weeks and would take up the whole day. I would go in the morning just after eight and would come back late. Once the treatment was finished for the day, I would feel like a zombie on my way home. I would be weak and lightheaded. I needed help to walk too because I fell over on my own.

One night, I had a very bad turn. I felt like I was going to die. I had never felt pain like that before. I felt like my stomach was coming out and I had both diarrhoea and vomiting. I began to sweat and feel dizzy. 'This is my time to die,' I thought.

I couldn't call my two children because although they were not far from me, I couldn't even reach for my stick to bang on the floor. I prayed, 'Lord, if it is my time, I am ready to go with You.' Straight away the Holy Spirit spoke to me and I heard a voice saying, 'You shall not die, but live.' I was extremely weak, but I immediately remembered that Bible verse and was amazed when

I heard the voice. I got up and started looking for the scripture. I think it was about 10 pm when I started looking for it but I did not find it until about 3 am. The scripture was in Psalms and I read it almost daily after that. It was Psalm 118:17: 'I shall not die, but live, and declare the works of the LORD.'

I was so happy that I had found it and that God had given me a second chance. All the bad feelings that I had left me that night and I slept so well. The next morning, my granddaughter Chenae, who was only two and a half at the time, climbed up onto the bed, put her hand on my forehead and mumbled a prayer for me in her baby language. The only words I could understand were, '...healed in Jesus' name, amen.' It was the hand of God on my life. My job was not finished yet. God knew my destiny.

The radiotherapy went on every day for three weeks. I would have an ambulance or a cab come to pick me up and the treatment would take about three hours. When the nurse called me in for the treatment, I had to get undressed, put on a hospital gown and then I would lie on the couch while the machine was brought over to me. They would inject a dye into my hand, and then turn the machine on, positioning it over the area where I'd had the operation. A red light would come on over the area and stay there for about ten minutes. This treatment was followed by blood tests and it all made me very lethargic and drowsy.

One morning, I scratched my breast and my skin peeled off so badly that I had to have a dressing put on it every day. It was very painful. I found the doctors, nurses and patients at the hospital very friendly but thank God it is all over. As the songwriter says, 'To God be the glory, great things He has done.'

I would like to say to anyone going through a similar situation that God can carry you through it. A cancer diagnosis doesn't always mean that it is the end of the road for you so trust and believe in God. You will need your family and friends around you. Don't be ashamed or afraid to lean on your loved ones in this time of need. This will be a time you turn to the things you enjoy for comfort and distraction. For me, this meant singing and being around my loved ones more often. It is important to stay positive and surround yourself with positive people. In my lowest times, I would read my Bible, sing songs that would uplift me and spend time with my family. My biggest lesson from this time in my life was to remain focused and positive, trust in God and hold onto my faith because this was a time when my faith was severely tested.

## Third Mini Stroke

It was June 2009 and I was at home alone when I felt a numbness coming over my body. My hand and my face felt strange. I immediately called my workplace hospital for help. Sister Rose Trusty, the sister on duty in the outpatient department, answered the phone.

I tried to explain that I needed help and she asked, 'Is that Cameta?'

I managed to answer, 'Yes,' and she said that she was on her way. She turned up at the house within minutes with a wheelchair and a porter. I threw the keys down to her through the window and she came in and took me over to the hospital. Once I arrived there, I lost all sense of what was going on. I could see what they were doing, but couldn't understand what they were saying and I couldn't feel what they were doing to me.

The next thing I knew I had been transferred to St George's Hospital in Tooting. I was in the hospital for about four weeks. On my second day there I saw on the news that Michael Jackson had died. Once I had been discharged, I had to attend a centre in Broad Green where I would have to learn to read and write again, feed myself and have speech therapy. All thanks and praise go to God who has brought me through, because if help had been delayed any longer things would have been worse.

## Divorce

I received the official letter stating that my divorce had been finalised on 23rd June 2010. I was so shocked that I did not know what to do. I read the letter about three times, and I cried and cried. I felt that all hope was gone. I felt rejected and as if I was on a rubbish heap ready to be burnt. I felt like a failure and that I had let my children down.

I cried almost every day. I could not go to work and had to take time off. I didn't want to talk to anyone or see anyone, other than my two children and Andrea's daughter, my lovely granddaughter Chenae. They and the Word were the things that kept me going. Each night I would cry and when the pillow was wet, I would turn it over. I felt such a sense of loss that it was as if a member of my family had died and I wasn't ever going to see them again. Although I had known that it was coming, it still hurt tremendously when it was finalised.

This was when God gave me several Bible verses to help me out during this difficult time. One of them was 'Humble yourselves in the sight of the Lord, and He shall lift you up' (James 4:10).

I began to feel better and my son said, 'Mum, it is all for the better. At least there is no more pain and trouble with Dad. He will be out of your life.' The song came back to me that said, 'My hope is built on nothing less than Jesus' blood and righteousness; I dare not trust the sweetest frame, but wholly lean on Jesus' Name.' I especially loved the chorus which went, 'On Christ, the solid Rock, I stand; all other ground is sinking sand.'

My daughter encouraged me too by saying, 'Mum, you can do it. You don't need him anymore. Because of your life in Christ, you are going to make it. You are a good mum to us. God is going to work in your life and we will be fine.'

# CHAPTER SEVEN

# Saying
## GOOD-BYE

### Gentleman, Teacher, Father, Friend

My dad was a very strict Christian. He was always impeccably dressed. He was a man who always liked to be on time for everything. He did not play church; he meant every word that he spoke and he lived what he preached. If you were lucky, he might tell you a little joke sometime. He was a deacon in the church and he was well respected. He would help anyone in need whether it be financial or spiritual help. My father was a people's person, a man of dignity and principle. People would come to him from all around to ask him for advice.

My father and I were very good friends. He left me in Jamaica when I was very young but when I came to live with him a few years later I was very happy. Everything for him was about the Word of God and he taught me how to be a young lady.

One day, I came in from school and had to cook dinner for everyone. I was so scared. My dad came into the kitchen and asked me what was wrong. I told him that I was afraid to cook so he said, 'Practice makes perfect, so go ahead and cook.' I felt better after he'd said that because if I made a mistake it would be his fault! Everything was going well; I cooked the chicken, but the rice turned out like porridge. I told my dad and he said, 'Cam, you have tried. Just put some sugar and milk in it and call it rice pudding!' I cooked again after that and it went well, so my dad said to me, 'See? Practice makes perfect.' I became a chef later in life because of my dad's encouragement.

My dad taught me how to iron men's shirts and trousers until I became an expert at it. He said, 'When you get married, no man will take advantage of you.'

My dad was also the first person to teach me how to drive. He gave me a few lessons in his Ford Escort and once he felt I could drive straight he paid for my first five driving lessons with an instructor.

As I was growing up, my dad often had conversations with me to try and instil his wisdom into me. I remember one Saturday when I was about fifteen years old, my dad was doing some chores around the house before he would settle down to watch his wrestling on the telly. He was changing a fuse in a plug socket and when I asked him what he was doing he explained that the fuse had blown and he was changing it. He showed me what to do and explained that it was important to learn to do these things around the house like changing light bulbs and painting because it would help me to become independent.

In the late eighties around 1988, my dad decided that he wanted to go back to his home in Jamaica. My parents moved back to Jamaica for good during the winter of 1989. They bought a big eight-bedroom house there so that we would have somewhere to live if we wanted to come and live in Jamaica. My parents spent many years in Jamaica and as their children, we'd go and visit them on holiday.

On one of our holidays to Jamaica, my dad went to feed the cow and came back limping. When we asked him what had happened, he said that he was in pain and that we should not come near him. A little later he called my mum and asked her to look at his foot. When she went to look at it, she saw that his big toe was swollen. His toe was huge! She asked him what had happened and he said that he had kicked the cow. We all wanted to laugh but we couldn't do it around him.

I remember that he used to take two spoons, sit on the veranda and then using the spoons as a musical instrument, he would play a tune and sing.

My dad became very ill one day so we took him to the doctor to do tests. The results came back and he was diagnosed with prostate cancer. Whenever I spoke to him on the phone, I would ask him how he was doing but my dad never complained. Even when he was in pain, he would say, 'I'm doing good.'

My brother Wayne was living in Jamaica at the time so he was the one who was caring for my dad. It was extremely difficult for Wayne but he looked after him with love. Dad's health deteriorated and things became hard for him so I took some time off work to go and help Wayne to look after my dad. This also allowed Wayne to have a little break. My sister Pauline and I went to Jamaica. I took a suitcase of medication for my dad because it was so expensive in Jamaica.

When I arrived and saw my dad I couldn't stop crying. I noticed at once how much weight he had lost but he was still as cheerful as ever.

'Hi, Dad,' I said and he replied, 'You come?'

'Yes, Dad, and Pauline, and your grandson Sean.'

He looked at Sean and smiled, 'Nice baby.'

Wayne filled me in on how our father was doing and how many times a day his dressings needed to be changed, which was twice. The next morning, I had to give him breakfast and get him dressed. I went into his room, got everything ready and greeted him. 'Good morning, Dad.'

'Is it morning already?' he asked.

'Yes, Dad, and I've come to get you ready for the day.'

He laughed and said, 'Okay, Miss, go ahead.'

When I started to take off the dressing, I was shocked. His wound was really bad. I thought one side of his bottom was gone. I couldn't believe it. The smell was so bad I wondered how Wayne did it day in, day out. After dressing him, I had to make up the bed so I told him I would roll him to the one side. When I did, my dad saw himself in the mirror and said, 'Cam, you are looking after a dead man.'

'No, Dad, you are very much alive,' I told him.

It was painful for me to look after him for just a short while, but Wayne had been doing this every day for months.

Each morning I looked after him and when we were finished my dad and I would sing. One of his favourite songs was 'Jesus, keep me near the cross, There a precious fountain, Free to all, a healing stream, Flows from Calvary mountain. In the Cross, in the Cross, be my glory ever, Till my rapture soul shall find rest beyond the river.'

Another of his favourite songs was 'There is a land that is fairer than day', and the chorus said, 'In the sweet by and by, we shall meet on that beautiful shore. In the sweet by and by, we shall meet on that beautiful shore.'

My dad and I talked about the past a lot during this time and I thanked him for all he had done for me, especially for helping me with the rice that had turned into porridge! I was glad that I could look after him for a short time and I really take my hat off to Wayne who did it for so much longer.

The day came when I had to return to London. I called Wayne and he thanked me for looking after our dad. I told him that I loved him and he said, 'hehe' which meant yes.

One morning in 1998, Wayne called and told me that Dad had had a dream. He had dreamt before that he had been to a beautiful garden with so much light. There was a man at the gate who'd said to my dad, 'We are expecting you but you are early.' Well, a few weeks later, my dad dreamt the same dream but this time when he went to the gate, the man opened the gate and let him in. I talked to my dad the following Monday morning and he told me that he was going to be with the Lord. The very next morning Wayne called to tell me that Dad had passed away. It was the 17th of June 1998. He was 75 years old.

When my dad died, I was devastated. He had been the backbone of the family, the person I would go to for advice because he seemed like he could fix anything. I was happy that he was out of pain but terribly sad that he had gone.

How would I cope without him? I wondered. This was for sure something I thought I would never get over. I would think about him all the time, and sometimes I would sit quietly and just remember him, the things he would say, the jokes he would tell. I would have dreams about him, and sometimes they felt so real it would bring tears to my eyes. Of course, time eased the loss and God reminded me of the happy times Dad and I had had together. I was so very grateful for the special privilege of being able to care for him at the end.

## My Handsome Nephew

My nephew Neville's death probably shocked me the most, because it was so out of the blue. I was used to getting phone calls of him being taken to hospital, but never did I expect a call that he had passed away. He died when he was just 33, on the 8th of April 2000. It was a shock to my system as he had been like a son to me. It took me many years to come to terms with his passing.

I had met Neville when I had come to London to live with my parents. Neville was my older sister (Valerie's) son. He was the first of my parents' grandchildren to be born in London. He was a handsome little boy with lovely long hair. I had thought he was a girl at first! He was so cute that I fell in love with him. I looked after Neville as if he was my little brother. His mum was working in High Wycombe at the time, so he lived with us for a while. Neville was sick as a child. He had been diagnosed with chronic asthma and was in and out of the hospital. He grew into a nice young man who was full of humour and who loved to sing. He held many jobs, but he loved cooking so he went into catering for some time. He also started singing in churches and anywhere else that he would go. He became a member of The London Gospel Community Choir. Since he had a passion for singing, he used to perform at weddings and other functions and would be out most weekends performing all over England.

One Saturday morning, Neville went to the shop. On the way back, he took shelter in a phone box near his house because it had started to rain. He called me from there and told me that he wasn't feeling too well.

A few hours later, two police officers showed up at my house looking for my sister. They then proceeded to tell me that Neville had passed away on his way to St Thomas' Hospital. I couldn't understand what they were saying. I had just spoken to him that morning. I couldn't believe it.

They explained that he'd had an asthma attack at home and had gone outside his house for air when his neighbour had seen him and called the ambulance. They had given him CPR but he had passed away in the ambulance on his way to the hospital. I rushed to the hospital, and was able to see him. He looked as if he was asleep and was still warm. I kept wondering if they were really sure he had died. I was so confused and my mind was all over the place. It was as if I could see people talking but couldn't hear anything. Seeing Neville lying there didn't make sense and I kept asking if they were sure that he was dead.

Neville was a bit of a prankster and would often offend people with his jokes and pranks. A few weeks before he passed away, he'd started calling people to apologise. This was unlike him. I remember asking him why he was calling people and he said that he wanted to be free and at peace with everyone because sometimes his jokes would offend people when that was never really his intention.

Neville had two favourite songs: 'Jesus, You're the Centre of my Joy' and 'Blessed Assurance'. His funeral was like a concert. There were several different choirs there who gave tributes. It was held in my church which holds about 600 plus people and yet it was packed. I remember being in Jamaica on holiday one day after Neville had passed away. I was watching a gospel concert when I saw them performing his favourite songs! I was grateful to God for this happy reminder of him.

## We Only Have One Mother

The year 2001 saw another loss in my family. My mum passed away in April of that year at the age of 72. I was heartbroken because my mum and I had been best friends. Her death was sudden and certainly wasn't something I was expecting. For a long time afterward, I'd pick up the phone to call her and then remember that she wasn't there anymore.

We could talk about anything. We both had a good sense of humour. Sometimes in church my mum would get up to go to the toilet and as she'd walk past me, she would say, 'That man's head is so big!' and then I would laugh, but I dared not let my dad see me or I would get in trouble. My mum loved food, clothes and helping others and so do I.

Mum was a very strict Christian. She was like a prophet in the church and whatever she said would come true. Anytime we saw her get up in church and say, 'Thus said the Lord,' we would start to shake in our boots, especially if we knew that we were not right with God.

My mum loved the Lord and she loved to sing. Her favourite songs were, 'I am dwelling in the mountain where the golden sunlight gleams, o'er a land whose wondrous beauty far exceeds my fondest dreams' and 'I must have the Saviour with me, for I dare not walk alone, I must feel His presence near me, And His arm around me thrown'.

My mum was the Ladies' President, Sunday School Teacher, Prayer Team Leader, and Team Leader for the witnessing group at church. She was loved by all the church members, her friends and family. When I was going through problems, my mum was always there for me. She would pray with me, give me Bible verses to read and we would talk every day.

When my marriage was in trouble, my mum reminded me of what she had told me at the beginning – that I was going to have problems – and I sure did, but thank God she was there in my time of need. I would cry and complain to my mum and sometimes I would think it was too much for her but when I did not call her, she would call to see if I was all right.

When my dad passed away, the family decided that my mum should come to London for a while so she came and stayed with me and my family in 1999. She shared a room with Andrea and would wake up early in the mornings and just sit there looking and thinking. I remember one day Andrea asked me if she was okay, as she found it weird to wake up and have her gran just sitting there watching her.

Mum was diabetic and had two episodes where her blood sugar level went very low while she was staying with me. The first time, I was home with my mum and she was watching the TV in the front room. When I went to check on her, I asked her if she was okay and she didn't respond. Her eyes were open but she wasn't responding. I knew straight away that something was wrong. I realised immediately that it must be her blood sugar level and ran to get her some Lucozade. I started feeding it to her and she started to drink it. Once she was coming around, I gave her one of her diabetic sweets and then she was fine.

The second time was when she was asleep. I went to wake her up from her nap as she had been sleeping longer than expected but when I tried to wake her there was no response. Paul and I tried everything to wake her up but she wouldn't come around. We called an ambulance and they came and took her to the hospital. They said she was going into a coma as her blood sugar level had dropped very low. She was admitted for a few days and then she came out fine.

Mum had lived in Jamaica for almost three years without my father. During that time, I would speak to her a few times a week. Then one April in 2001 I called her and she said she hadn't been feeling too well. She explained that she was having chest pains, and I told her it could be angina, which was something she'd had before. I told her that Andrea and I would be coming to Jamaica to see her but she said, 'I will be gone by the time you get here.' I answered, 'No, Mum, we will see you soon.'

That conversation was on a Saturday night. On the Monday morning I got a phone call at work telling me that I needed to come home. When I got home, my son met me at the door and told me that my mum had passed away from a heart attack.

I told him, 'No, she hasn't. I spoke to her on Saturday.'

Then Paul said, 'Yes, your brother Wayne called to let us know,' and as he finished his sentence the phone rang and it was my brother Wayne again. He explained that he'd had a convention at his church that Mum wanted to go to. She hadn't been feeling too well though so Wayne had suggested that she stay home with the helper but she had insisted on going. While there she had given a testimony. She said the church should be prepared for the coming of Lord and that everyone should be prepared to meet Him. However, the helper who had gone to church with them noticed that my mum wasn't looking right. She told my brother and he told her to give mum one of her diabetic sweets, but it didn't seem to be helping. Mum had gone grey, clammy and sweaty.

They rushed her to the hospital. She was having very bad pains in her chest. My brother Wayne went home to get some of mum's bits and pieces as they were admitting her. As he was re-entering the hospital, he heard a scream. It was Mum. The doctor told him, 'If you want to see your mum, come now,' so Wayne rushed into the room just as Mum let out another scream. Wayne arrived in time to see her take her last breath. It was all over. Mum was out of pain.

I made arrangements to go to Jamaica with my family immediately and we were there within a week. I helped to make the funeral arrangements and we all gave my mother a great send-off. After that, it was time to leave again and make our way back to England. I hadn't cried throughout the whole thing so my sisters were wondering if I was okay. Once I was on the plane and I heard the pilot say we had ten minutes before landing, I started crying. I realised that I could no longer call my mum to say that I had landed safely. That was when it hit me very hard. My best friend had gone. I wouldn't see or hear her again. The only things that could comfort me were our memories and her favourite songs. Even today, those songs of hers are a blessing to me.

Mum, may you rest in the arms of God and I hope to meet you, Dad, and Neville in heaven one day.

## Farewell, My Dearest Friend

Lorraine Thompson was my best friend who also became my sister-in-law. Later, she came to be Andrea's godmother, too. We grew up together in church during the days of Sunday School and she was always a happy person who dispensed wise advice. Lorraine always had a smile on her face, was a good listener and was always willing to pray for you.

It was a shock when she became ill, and I had thought she would pull through it like I had but God had other plans and He knows best. She passed away from cancer in Jamaica on the 20th of July 2018 and was just 59 years old. She will always be in my heart. May her soul rest in peace.

Experiencing three of my family members passing away as well as my very best friend has been hard. I went through a lot of difficult and unexpected emotions at each passing. I felt overwhelmed each time, would ask a lot of questions and things still didn't seem to make sense. Still, this is a part of life that we must all go through. I have learnt to be grateful for the times and experiences we had together and the memories we made, and will always hold on to the good times.

I know that each one of them will forever live on in my heart, and they are always in my thoughts. Life is short and I don't take anyone or anything for granted. I have learnt that it is important to deal with my grief. It is important that I talk about it and how I am feeling as this can help others, as well as myself. If at any time I felt that I couldn't talk, I would write it down, but most importantly I needed to go through the grieving process and understand that it was okay to take as long as I needed. The Scriptures say in Psalm 55 verse 22: 'Cast thou thy burdens upon the Lord and He shall sustain thee, He shall never suffer the righteous to be moved.' This verse, in particular, helped me through those difficult times of loss and grief.

# CHAPTER EIGHT

# Faith
## AND HOPE

'My faith looks up to Thee, Thou Lamb of Calvary, Saviour divine; Now hear me while I pray, Take all my guilt away; Oh, let me from this day, be wholly Thine!' – Redemption song.

What have a learnt on the road I have walked so far? That without faith, it is impossible to please God and it is only because of my faith that I am still here. I have to trust and believe in God that He will supply all my needs. I have to dedicate time to fasting and prayer. I have to pray with power and conviction, knowing that God will answer my prayers. I believe that it strengthens my faith when I see my prayers being answered.

I have been through the mill but God was there for me all the time, through the good and the bad times. Because of the things I've experienced, people often ask me to pray for them and it sometimes surprises me, as some of the people that ask are pastors, deacons and other church leaders. They ask me to pray because of my faith, and because they know and have seen how God has answered my prayers.

I have prayed for people who have needed jobs and homes and for people to be healed from their illness. No matter the situation, when I pray I believe that God is going to answer. He said, 'Make your requests known and I will do whatsoever I say I will do.'

I pray for them and say, 'Lord Jesus, I come to You in no other name but in the name of Jesus. I thank You for who You are. You are my saviour and my friend. A God that sticks closer than a brother. Now, Lord, I come to you undone. I need you to forgive me of my sins. Jesus, You know me inside out. I am trusting and believing in You, so I leave this situation totally in Your hands. I give it to You Lord, in no other name but in the name of Jesus.'

When I pray those prayers God must answer because when I read the Word it says in Philippians 4:6, 'Be careful for nothing; but in everything, by prayer and supplication with thanksgiving, let your requests be made known unto God.' This is what I do and I see the results.

I was at home one day when I got a phone call asking me to come and pray for a church sister who was ill. When I arrived at her house, she described the pain she was feeling and said that she had tried everything she could think of to ease it. She had taken medication and home remedies. She had also prayed but the pain wasn't going away.

I put my hands on her stomach where she said that the pain was and I prayed a prayer from my heart that God would heal her from the terrible pain she was experiencing. The next day she called and told me that she had recovered, so I gave thanks to God because it was not me, but God who had healed her. That is what faith in God can do. The Bible says in James 5:15, 'And the prayer of faith shall save the sick and the Lord shall raise him up, and if he has committed sins, they shall be forgiven him.' Amen.

There have been many times in my life when my faith has seen me through. Throughout my strokes, my cancer, my asthma attacks, my divorce, my son's illnesses, the decision to leave England to go and live in Jamaica and return from Jamaica to start life over again in the UK, in my jobs, and in my entire life's walk I have always prayed and believed that God would answer my prayer. This is what it means to have faith in God. Through faith, I received my strength.

God gave me a second chance so that I could live again and I thank Him for it. From the safety pin that was lodged in my spine in 2005 which rendered me unable to move, to the breast cancer, minor strokes and asthma diagnosis of 2010, I can clearly see how God's grace and my faith have brought me this far. Had it not been for my faith I would surely have died. Thank God He never changes. James 2:26 says, 'For as the body without the spirit is dead, so faith without works is dead also.'

When you put all your trust in God, He will show up for you. I am also reminded of James 5:16 where the last line in the verse reads, 'The effectual fervent prayer of the righteous man availeth much.' This shows just how important our prayers are. No matter what you are going through, if you are a child of God, He is there with you.

The Bible says in Hebrews 11:1, 'Now faith is the substance of things hoped for, the evidence of things not seen.' We cannot see everything yet we believe. That is faith and that's what I hold on to because faith without works is dead. If you pray, fast and read the Word, you can never go wrong. God's Word is the truth and we can only overcome by reading and believing it. Each morning when I wake up, I have to give God thanks first, before I say anything else. I have to keep looking to God because He is the author and finisher of my faith. Faith is a gift from God.

I remember that many times I had to stretch my faith but didn't realise that I was doing that until I looked back and saw what I had gone through. It was only God testing me and I didn't know it at the time. My faith was tested like Abraham's.

## Prayer of Faith

When my son Dean was about twelve years old, he became very sick – he had high temperatures, cramps in his stomach, vomiting and diarrhoea and couldn't keep down anything he ate at all.

The doctors could not find what was wrong with him at first. They told me that there was not much they could do for him so I came home, went down on my knees and cried out to God. I prayed, 'God, You have to do something for me.' I went into my bathroom and dialled Heaven.

It was a very difficult time for me when my son was ill like that. My husband was in St Thomas' Hospital at the time, and Dean was in Mayday Hospital so I had two family members to pray for. I needed help immediately. I needed an answer from God for my son so that the doctors could find out what was wrong with him. I remember that one evening I went home to pray but I was interrupted by a phone call from the hospital. It was a nurse saying that Dean wanted to talk to me. They put him on the phone, and he said, 'Mum I'm going to pray and ask God to let the doctors find what is wrong with me.'

I answered, 'Dean I am in agreement with you. We will both pray.' We said goodnight to each other knowing that God was going to answer our prayers because we believed His Word. Dean was young but he had known about God from an early age so he knew how to pray.

When I came off the phone, I went down on my knees and prayed, 'Lord, here is Your daughter, I need Your help and my help comes from You who made the heavens and the earth. God, You see these two situations I have before me. I leave them in Your hands. Father, You alone can change them.'

The next morning, I went to see Dean before I went on hospital duty (I worked in that same hospital in the main outpatient department). Dean told me that he'd had a dream that the doctor had come in to see him, and on the table, there had been a brown envelope. Inside that envelope had been written the condition that he'd been diagnosed with. When I heard of the dream I exclaimed, 'God has answered our prayers!'

Dean was so sick that we took it in turns between myself and

Andrea to sleep at the hospital with him. About two days after we had prayed, the doctor called me to come into the ward where Dean was and I went in faith, knowing that God had answered our prayers because my faith has never disappointed me.

The Bible says in Matthew 17:20b, 'If ye have faith as a grain of mustard seed, ye shall say unto this mountain, Remove hence to yonder place and it shall remove, and nothing shall be impossible unto you.'

This is what I believed. Faith tells me that I can do all things through Christ who strengthens me (Philippians 4:13). Faith tells me to never doubt but just believe because whatever you ask in faith, God will do.

When I went to the ward, the doctor spoke to Dean and me. 'I have good news,' he said. Just as Dean had dreamt it, I saw a brown envelope on the table. The doctor picked up the envelope, opened it and began to read. He then explained that Dean had Crohn's disease and that it could be controlled by treatment, which would hopefully stop the symptoms coming back. I said, in front of the doctor, 'Thank You, Jesus, for answering our prayers.' I hugged Dean and thanked the doctor.

So, you can see that when you stretch your faith, God works. This was the evidence of things not seen yet believed. Amen. If you cannot walk, faith tells you that you can. If you cannot see, faith tells you that you can see. If you are sick, faith tells you that you can be healed. If you are weak, faith tells you that you are strong. My husband left the hospital on the very same day that Dean received his results. Hebrews 13:8 says, 'Jesus Christ is the same yesterday and today and forever.' God cannot go back on His Word which is why I believe Him fully.

Through it all, I have learned to trust in Jesus, and I have learned to trust in God! This is faith. Sometimes when I think of faith, I am reminded of my grandmother. You might remember that in Chapter One I told you a story about her faith. One day, when I was six years old, my grandmother called my siblings and me to come into the yard. She said that we needed to pray because she didn't have any dinner to give us. We had all gathered around while my grandmother had prayed and I remember believing that God would send us some dinner that night. Once she had finished praying, she'd told my sister Pauline to put a pot on the fire with water in and fill it up. We had all wondered why she was doing this as she'd just said she didn't have any food to cook. Pauline had done as she'd been told and put the pot of water on to boil. After some time, she'd told my granny that the water was drying out and my gran had replied, 'Fill it up again,' and Pauline had done that.

An hour later a friend of my granny's had come by the house with a basket on his head and said, 'Ms Richards, I come to bring you this basket of food from my ground (allotment).' When my grandmother had looked, there had been yams, potatoes, green bananas, sweet potatoes, dasheens, and callaloo. I remember that my grandmother had lifted her hands and started praising God. I realise now that this was true faith. My grandmother had believed that God would send us some food to eat and He surely had.

Of course, there have been times in my life when my faith has wavered but only for a short while. These were mainly in times of sickness, when Dean was ill and they couldn't find what was wrong with him, and when I was diagnosed with cancer. There would be a day or two when I wondered why it was happening to me, but despite those times, I'd continued to pray without ceasing and had soon found my faith again.

## Gambia

One of my most memorable experiences of exercising my faith was when I got the chance to visit Gambia. My friends Audrey and George Thompson went to Gambia on holiday and told me all about it when they got back. Their son had visited before them and had told them how beautiful and peaceful it was there. They liked it so much that they bought a house out there and once they had settled in, they invited me to come over on holiday.

I went in October 2017 at the end of the rainy season. I was interested to visit an orphanage there that they had told me about. They had come across it one day when George had been going somewhere and his car had become stuck in the mud. It had taken him four hours to get out of it, and some young boys had helped him. When he had dropped them home, he'd noticed a sign saying, 'Grace House'. He learnt that this was a Christian orphanage. The orphanage had been started ten years earlier by a team of South Korean missionaries.

The Koreans had no longer been able to support the ministry and the new owner was a man called Ebrima. He and his wife were quite concerned about the future. At that time, Ebrima and his wife had two children of their own and twenty-seven orphans. George and Audrey were able to fill the gap for a year and help them out. George and Audrey had prayed about how they could continue to help the orphanage. They had used their own money as well as money from others. The church that George attended in England helped, and his mother's church helped also.

When I was told about this orphanage in Gambia, I wanted to help in any way that I could. My heart always went out to those who did not have much. Even when I used to see people who had no food or water on the TV, I would cry for them. I remember one time saying to my mum, 'One day I will help those people.' I didn't know at the time that God would make a way for me to help.

I got to meet Ebrima, his wife, their children and the orphans. I could see that they needed many things. The first thing I realised was that they needed drinking water. They had a well but it was almost dry. I asked them where they got their water from and Ebrima said that it was far away and the road was bad, so sometimes they lost most of the water on the way back.

I was also able to visit another couple who lived in a mud house. They invited me in but I couldn't stay for very long as there was so much dust inside and it was stuffy with no windows. I didn't want to trigger my asthma. The lady brought out a chair for me to sit on. It was bent and had a hole in the seat so she put a cloth over it for me. I knew that this was their best chair and the tears just ran down my face. George knew that they needed food so he bought them a bag of rice.

Wherever we went in Gambia there were a lot of children. George would buy sweets for them. Even the adults would want sweets and they started to call George 'Minty'. They'd recognise his car anywhere they saw it.

While I was in Gambia, we went to visit a friend one day. We saw about four boys there each with a dead rabbit slung over their arm. As they got closer to us, I realised that they were not rabbits at all, but were, in fact, rats! They were taking them home to cook. It was explained to me that this was called 'bush meat' and they would eat it with rice.

I also had the opportunity to visit the school. There were so many children that the staff were trying to extend it. It was a Muslim school but the religious education teacher was also teaching them about Christianity.

I was so concerned and touched by what I had learnt in Gambia that I started to think about how I could help. I came back to England with two things on my mind. One was to help the orphanage to obtain clean drinking water, and the second was to help the family in the mud house. As soon as I got back to England, I started planning a concert to raise money for the people in Gambia. I asked all of my family and friends to help with whatever they could give. I asked the doctors and nurses that I work with and sold tickets for the concert. Between the concert and the other churches collecting in the UK, we raised enough money for the orphanage to be able to get a water pump. Now the orphanage has running water. They can help others and are now growing their own food and looking after livestock. The orphanage also now has flushing toilets. Things are looking up for the orphanage. Thank God for friends and family who have a willing heart to help!

I received a monetary gift for the couple who lived in the mud house. With the money, they were able to start rebuilding their house using cement, and they had windows put in, too. They no longer have to worry about their house being washed away when there is heavy rain. The people in Gambia do not ask for much. They work with the little you give them. I thank God for the change in the orphanage, the school and the couple living in the mud house.

The orphanage, Grace House, is doing well, and Ebrima and his wife are managing to keep the children fed and in school. They have daily Bible devotions at the orphanage, church on Sundays, and an afterschool Bible study at the predominantly Muslim school every Friday. Some of George and Audrey's other friends and churches are also helping.

Please join us in praying for Ebrima and his wife and the daily challenges they face supporting their extended family. I will continue to help them and others who are in need, but we hope that one day they will be self-sufficient. I thank Audrey and George for telling me about the help needed there and inviting me to Gambia. Whatever little help we can give to others let us do it and do it in love, because God loves a cheerful giver.

When I look back on my life and all the memories and lessons learnt, I am thankful for all the good and the hard times as they have made me who I am today. I am so grateful for my children and grandchildren who have helped and encouraged me to grow as a person. I am thankful for my family and friends, for without their love and support this book wouldn't be possible.

God will always be my rock, no matter what the situation. I have found a friend in Jesus, and He is always with me. He will never leave me nor forsake me. He has become, my saviour, my deliverer and my peace. Nothing is impossible with God – I've seen that over my life. I therefore challenge you all to put your trust in God, and see the changes He can make in your life, too. Trust in the Lord with all thine heart, and lean not unto thine own understanding, in all thy ways acknowledge him and he shall direct thy path. (Proverbs 3 v 5-6)

# About
## THE AUTHOR

Cameta Senior was born in Jamaica and came to live in the UK in 1968 at the age of 10. Her passion is to see women healed of wounds from negative experiences in their past so they can walk in the full liberty Christ came to give them.

Today she speaks to women at conferences, churches and events to help them overcome their fears, trauma and wounds. She mentors women, is part of several prayer groups and initiatives, and also takes part in prison ministries.

If you would like contact Cameta, email info@roadshewalks.com

Printed in Great Britain
by Amazon